KT-428-161

CAMRA'S

BEER

Knowledge

ESSENTIAL WISDOM FOR
THE DISCERNING DRINKER

Jeff Evans

CAMRA

BOOKS

Published by the Campaign for Real Ale Ltd.
230 Hatfield Road
St Albans
Hertfordshire AL1 4LW

www.camra.org.uk/books

Design and layout © Campaign for Real Ale 2016
Text © Jeff Evans
First published 2004
Reprinted with updates and amendments 2007
Second edition 2011, reprinted 2014
Third edition published 2016

ISBN 978-1-85249-338-7

A CIP catalogue record for this book is available from the British Library.
Printed and bound in Poland by Latitude Press Ltd

Head of Publishing: Simon Hall
Project Editor: Katie Button
Editorial Assistance: Emma Haines
Design/Typography: Linda Storey, Top Floor Design Ltd
Sales & Marketing: David Birkett

Picture credits: cover (top left) Strejman/Shutterstock;
p4, p146 Alexander_P/Shutterstock

Introduction

Welcome to the third edition of CAMRA's *Beer Knowledge*.

The success of this book, I confess, has taken me a little by surprise. I thoroughly enjoyed compiling the first two editions – it's a labour of love – but I didn't realise that quite so many people shared my fascination with facts, figures and feats.

This latest edition includes some old favourites – lists of the biggest, the most, the best, etc. – all fully updated, but it also packs in many new items that I hope readers will find informative, intriguing or preferably both.

Once again, insights into the sillier side of beer rub shoulders with serious statistics. In the following pages, you will find the most common beer names, the countries that grow the most hops, the best-selling beer brands and the cheapest cities for beer, plus information about subjects as diverse as beer styles, heritage pubs, taxation and beers served in restaurants, planes and trains – all mixed up with a smattering of history, awards results and some typically daft stories from the world of beer.

What I have aimed to produce is a miscellany of beer information that I hope will be seen as a combination of handy reference work and a book for light-hearted browsing.

If it proves as popular as the last two editions, there may be more to follow. Any suggestions for lists and items to include will, as always, be very welcome and can be forwarded to me via CAMRA using the following email address: books@camra.org.uk.

Jeff Evans

The World's Biggest Brewers

The giants: the companies that produce the most beer around the world.

	Company	Million hl
1	AB InBev	411.5
2	SABMiller	187.8
3	Heineken	181.3
4	Carlsberg	122.8
5	China Resources Snow Breweries	118.4
6	Tsingtao Brewery Group	76.2
7	Molson Coors	59.0
8	Yanjing	53.1
9	Kirin	46.6
10	BGI/Groupe Castel	31.7
11	Efes Group	24.5
12	Petropolis	21.8
13	Asahi	20.7
14	Gold Star	19.1
15	Polar	17.7
16	Diageo (Guinness)	17.5
17	San Miguel Corporation	16.7
18	Singha Corporation	15.8
19	Saigon Beverage Corp. (SABECO)	13.0
20	Grupo Mahou – San Miguel	12.1

Figures given are for 2013, prior to the proposed AB InBev takeover of SABMiller.
Source: *British Beer & Pub Association Statistical Handbook 2015*.

Political Pint Scoring

In an online poll conducted by YouGov for CAMRA ahead of the 2016 Great British Beer Festival, British adults were asked which politician they would trust most to run a local pub. Out of a list of likely candidates, including Theresa May and Jeremy Corbyn, the winner was Boris Johnson, with more than one in five respondents declaring that the former Mayor of London would be their choice to pull pints and lend a sympathetic ear across the bar. Johnson narrowly pushed Nigel Farage into second place.

The Fabulous Five

The *Good Beer Guide* is CAMRA's flagship publication. For more than 40 years it has led British beer-lovers to pubs serving the best traditional ale and provided details about the country's breweries and the beers they produce. However, only five pubs have now featured in every edition.*

Buckingham Arms, Westminster, London SW1
Queen's Head, Newton, Cambridgeshire
Roscoe Head, Liverpool, Merseyside
Square & Compass, Worth Matravers, Dorset
Star Tavern, Belgravia, London SW1

* To 2017 edition.

Burglar's Bud Mistake

Police admit that they might never have caught burglar Andrew Gibney if he hadn't been quite so thirsty. In 2012, having raided the Black Dog pub in Newent, Gloucestershire, along with three accomplices, and stealing nearly £1,800 in cash, getaway driver Gibney cracked open a purloined bottle of Budweiser. But, when he abandoned the empty bottle outside, police were able to trace him through the DNA left on the glass. The others got clean away but Gibney was jailed for 27 months after admitting the crime (the burglary, not the drinking of a Budweiser).

The Greeks Had a Word For It

Symposium, today, is a posh word for a formal meeting or conference at which experts exchange views on serious subjects. But it wasn't always like that. In ancient Greece, a symposium was actually a drinking party, at which men imbibed, conversed and had a bit of a laugh. So, the next time you are in need of an excuse to head for the pub, try explaining that you are simply attending a symposium. It might just get a better reception.

Rock & Roll Beers

Beer and rock music are natural bedfellows and, as if to prove this, an increasing number of musicians are now collaborating with breweries to produce their own commercial brews, among them the following beers.

Artist(s)	Beer	Brewery
AC/DC	Rock or Bust	Karlsberg (D)
Elbow	build a rocket boys!	Robinsons
	Charge	Marston's
Grateful Dead	American Beauty	Dogfish Head (US)
Hanson	Mmmhops	Mustang (US)
Idlewild	Scottish Fiction IPA	Barney's
Iron Maiden	Trooper	Robinsons
	Trooper 666	Robinsons
	Trooper Red 'n' Black	Robinsons
Kid Rock	Badass American Lager	Brew Detroit (US)
Kiss	Destroyer	Krönleins (S)
Madness	Gladness	Growler*/Portobello
	Lovestruck	Portobello
	Nightboat	Portobello
Mastodon	Black Tongue	Signature Brew
Maximo Park	Maximo No.5	Mordue
Metallica	Budweiser Metallica	AB InBev (US)
Motörhead	Bastards	Krönleins (S)
Mumford & Sons	Lewes Stopover Brew	Harveys
New Order	Stray Dog	Moorhouse's
Pearl Jam	Faithfull Ale	Dogfish Head (US)
Professor Green	Remedy	Signature Brew
Queen	Bohemian Lager	Schwarzenberg (CZ)
Reverend & the Makers	Summer Ale	Thornbridge
	American Brown	Thornbridge
Slayer	666 Red Ale	Nils Oscar (S)
Status Quo	Dog of Two Head	Hobsons
	Piledriver	Wychwood
Stereophonics	Phonics	Brains

* Now known again as Nethergate.

Breweries are UK unless noted: D Germany, US USA, S Sweden, CZ Czech Republic.

Brewers of the Year (Part One)

Since 1995, the UK All-Party Parliamentary Beer Group has presented an annual award to its chosen 'Brewer of the Year'. Here is a list of winners.

Year	Brewer	Brewery
1995	Tony Skipper	McMullen
1996	Paul Bayley	Marston's
1997	Paul Theakston	Black Sheep
1998	Alistair Heeley	Greene King
1999	Reg Drury	Fuller's
2000	Stuart Noble	Bass
2001	Miles Jenner	Harveys
2002	Ken Don	Young's
2003	Mike Powell-Evans	Adnams
2004	Giles Dennis	Lees
2005	Jeremy Moss	Wychwood
2006	Steve Fielding	Thwaites
2007	Steve Wellington	White Shield
2008	Ian Dixon	Shepherd Neame
2009	Roger Ryman	St Austell
2010	Stefano Cossi	Thornbridge
2011	Stuart Howe	Sharp's
2012	Toby Heasman	Hall & Woodhouse
2013	Fergus Fitzgerald	Adnams
2014	Emma Gilleland	Marston's
2015	Alastair Hook	Meantime
2016	John Keeling	Fuller's

Brewery Misses a Beat

In the 1960s, a commercially-aware group of pop musicians in Birmingham decided to capitalise on the fact that they were getting bookings in pubs operated by the local brewery, Mitchells & Butlers. They called themselves the M&B Five to build up the liaison and approached the brewery in the hope of securing some sponsorship. None came and so the band decided to expand the initials into a proper name. When, as the Moody Blues, they scored their first hit, the brewery was left rueing a missed opportunity.

Brewers of the Year (Part Two)

Since 2005, the British Guild of Beer Writers has presented an award to its own choice of 'Brewer of the Year'. The recipients to date are as follows.

Year	Brewer	Brewery
2005	John Keeling	Fuller's
2006	Roger Ryman	St Austell
2007	Mike Powell-Evans	Adnams
2008	Alastair Hook	Meantime
2009	Miles Jenner	Harveys
2010	Stefano Cossi	Thornbridge
2011	Evan O'Riordain	Kernel
2012	Sara Barton	Brewster's
2013	Derek Prentice	Fuller's
2014	Mark Tranter	Burning Sky
2015	Jenn Merrick	Beavertown

Blasts from the Past

As well as looking to the future by experimenting with new hops, unusual ingredients and unconventional techniques, brewers are also now paying tribute to the past. Fuller's and Shepherd Neame are two companies that have sought to capitalise on their brewing heritage by recreating recipes from their own archives. Dusting off the brewing books, Fuller's launched its excellent Past Masters series in 2010, producing fascinating ales that have not been on sale for decades. It began with XX Strong Ale, based on a recipe from 1891, and followed this with Double Stout, dating from 1893, and Old Burton Extra from 1931. Later recreations include an oatmeal porter from 1926 and a ruby ale from 1966. Shepherd Neame introduced its Classic Collection in 2012. This was not as straightforward as first appears because, back in the day, Shepherd Neame brewing recipes were recorded in a special code, to make it impossible for a brewer to take a recipe to another brewery. The code duly unravelled, the Kent brewery was able to resurrect its own Double Stout – dating from 1868 – along with an India pale ale from 1870. It has since added Brilliant Ale – a sunny, golden beer – to the archive selection. Dating possibly from as early as 1825, it underlines that golden ales are not a modern invention.

Airline Beers

Arguably the best beers offered by international airlines (based on long-haul flights in economy: some airlines provide these free, others charge).

Aer Lingus	Dingle Crean's Lager
Air China	Yanjing Draft
Air New Zealand	Steinlager
Alitalia	Moretti speciality beers
American Airlines	Samuel Adams Boston Lager
Austrian Airlines	Ottakringer Helles
British Airways	St Austell Tribute
Cathay Pacific	San Miguel
Czech Airlines	Gambrinus
Delta Airlines	Sweetwater 420 Extra Pale Ale
easyJet	Greene King Old Speckled Hen
Emirates	Heineken
Eurowings	Warsteiner
Finnair	Karhu
Garuda	Bintang
Iberia	Mahou
Icelandair	Ölgerdin Gull
Japan Airlines	Sapporo Yebisu
KLM	Heineken
Lot Polish Airlines	Zywiec
Lufthansa	Warsteiner
Malaysian Airlines	Tiger
Monarch	Stella Artois
Norwegian	Heineken
Qantas	James Boag's Premium
Ryanair	Heineken
SAS	Mikkeller The Cloud Hopper
Singapore Airlines	Tiger
South African Airways	Hansa Pilsener
Swiss	Appenzeller Quöllfrisch
Thomas Cook	Stella Artois
Thomson	Stella Artois
United Airlines	Goose Island IPA
Virgin Atlantic	Tiger

Beers for Ageing

Most beers are designed to be drunk young and fresh but others can mature beautifully in the bottle. Here are some beers that, because of their strength, active yeast or other factors, are noted to improve in the bottle.

Alaskan Smoked Porter
Anchor Old Foghorn
Chimay Blue/Grand Réserve
Coopers Vintage Ale
De Dolle Stille Nacht
Drie Fonteinen Oude Gueze
Durham Temptation
Eggenberger Samichlaus
Fuller's Gale's Prize Old Ale
Fuller's Vintage Ale
Goose Island Bourbon County Stout
Harveys Imperial Extra Double Stout
Lees Harvest Ale
Old Chimneys Good King Henry Special Reserve
Orval
Pitfield 1896 XXXX Stock Ale
Rochefort 10
Rodenbach Grand Cru
Samuel Smith Yorkshire Stingo
Schneider Aventinus
Sierra Nevada Bigfoot Barleywine
Westvleteren 12/Abt

A 1970s Take on Keg Beer

'It's all piss and wind, like a barber's cat.'
– Customer in a West Midlands pub

Source: *The Death of the English Pub,* by Christopher Hutt (Arrow, 1973).

A Concise Guide to Traditional British Beer Styles

Mild   3–3.5%   **Amber to near-black**
Mild is available in dark and paler forms, both of which are malt- rather than hop-driven, with a restrained bitterness. Dark milds often have a roasted grain flavour. Stronger milds also exist, a legacy of the days when beer in Britain was generally more potent. Until the end of the 1950s, mild was the UK's most popular beer style.

Brown Ale   2.8–5%   **Amber to near-black**
Brown ales were once just milds in a bottle but have developed more of a defined character of their own, often with heavier hopping, thanks to the influence of American craft brewers. The southern style tends to be sweet and lower in strength; the northern (or more precisely north-eastern style) is generally more bitter and robust.

Bitter   2.5–4%   **Amber to brown**
Light- to medium-bodied with notable hop flavours and bitterness. Some sweetness and possibly nut or caramel may come from the malt; hops may bring citrus, herbal or floral notes. The beer that the rest of the world envies.

Best Bitter   4–5%   **Amber to brown**
Medium- to full-bodied with malt flavours such as nut or caramel supporting plenty of hop bitterness. A stronger, more substantial take on a bitter.

Golden Ale   3–5%   **Straw to deep golden**
Crisp and bittersweet, with only a delicate malt character and often pronounced citrus or floral hop flavours. Although many British ales were once golden or light amber in colour, darker beers gradually took over. This paler style has bounced back in popularity since the late 1980s, inspired by the success of golden lagers, and is now ubiquitous.

Burton Ale   5–8%   **Dark amber to brown**
A near-obsolete style of ale that has its origins in the Staffordshire town of the same name but disappeared from the public's gaze in the last half of the 20th century. Dark, relatively strong and fairly sweet, where it does exist it is often now labelled as a strong mild, old ale or winter warmer.

Strong Ale　　　　5% and up　　　Golden to dark brown

Chunky, malty beer with a balancing bitter hop character. Fermentation can introduce floral or fruity notes. May also be described as special ale or extra special ale.

India Pale Ale　　　4.8% and up　　Golden to deep amber

Robust and full-bodied with a pronounced hop character, which may be softly fruity if based on UK hops and strongly citrus or floral if New World hops are used. The beer that once quenched thirsts in Imperial India.

Old Ale　　　　　　4.5% and up　　Amber to near-black

Once a beer that was deliberately aged for months and then often served blended with fresh, young beer but mostly today a malt-forward, fruity, sometimes vinous strong ale, with a low bitterness and sometimes with notes of chocolate.

Barley Wine　　　　7% and up　　　Golden to brown

A substantial, strong ale with a full malt profile and at least enough hops for balance, although sweetness may dominate. Tropical fruit from the fermentation process can be expected and winey notes may develop as the beer ages.

Stout and Porter　　3% and up　　　Amber to near-black

Stout was once simply a stronger version of porter and there's often not much to choose between them today. Contemporary porter tends to be a little lighter in body and perhaps more sweet and chocolatey than stout, which can be dry and bitter with a strong roasted grain character. But then there are sweet stouts and milk stouts, the latter containing lactose for creamy body. Oatmeal stouts may have a slight porridge creaminess, while imperial stouts and Baltic porters – once brewed for export – are big beasts packed with alcohol, malt and hops that can be vinous.

Scottish Ale　　　　3% and up　　　Ruby to dark brown

Scottish beer, traditionally, has had a malt accent, which means darker, sweeter brews with notes of caramel and toffee to the fore. But against this backdrop beers have been subdivided, ranging widely in strength from Light (the equivalent of mild) through Heavy (best bitter) to Export (IPA or strong ale). Today's Scottish brewers, however, are not hamstrung by tradition and are as adventurous as any when it comes to beer recipes.

Capital Beer: Paris

Five great beer bars to check out on your next visit to the French capital.

Le Bouillon Belge, 6 rue Planchat, 75020
This bar can be found in the east of the city, near Place de la Nation, and, as the name suggests, it majors on Belgian beer, with around a hundred bottles to try.

Brewberry, 11 rue du Pot-de-Fer, 75005
Twenty-four draught beers feature in this Latin Quarter bar – a spin-off from a beer shop – near the Panthéon.

L'Express de Lyon, 1 rue de Lyon, 75012
Traditional bar handy for the Gare de Lyon, serving beers from Europe's trendiest breweries and small French brewers.

La Fine Mousse, 6 Avenue Jean Aicard, 75011
Artisanal beer house with 20 taps and loads of bottles (many French) near Père Lachaise cemetery.

Les Trois 8, 11 rue Victor Letalle, 75020
Bustling bar with bare-brick walls, eight draught beers and loads of bottles, also close to Père Lachaise.

Craft Brewer – a US Definition

According to the Brewers Association, an American craft brewer is small, independent and traditional, although, as the industry has developed, the precise qualifying terms have been modified. Here are the latest criteria.

Small: annual production amounts to 6 million US barrels of beer or less.

Independent: less than 25% of the brewery is owned or controlled by an alcoholic beverage industry member that is not itself a craft brewer.

Traditional: the majority of its beer output derives its flavour from traditional or innovative brewing ingredients and their fermentation.

The Most Common Beer Names

Many beers are simply named after colours, hop varieties or traditional beer styles, but it seems great minds think alike as there are a number of other names now repeatedly being used by UK brewers for their cask ales.

Beer Name	No. of Breweries	Beer Name	No. of Breweries
Dark Horse	10	Golden Fleece	3
Original	9	HPA	3
Classic	6	Hurricane	3
Pure Gold	6	Mucky Duck	3
Black Gold	5	Natural Blonde	3
Red Kite	5	Nemesis	3
Blondie	4	Northern Lights	3
Dark Knight	4	Pheasant Plucker	3
Dark Matter	4	Premium	3
Original Bitter	4	Rambler	3
Ruby Red	4	Red Squirrel	3
Sunshine	4	Resolution	3
Triple Hop	4	Saxon Gold	3
Centurion	3	Session	3
Eclipse	3	Sundowner	3
Elderflower Blonde	3	Traditional	3
Gold Rush	3	Warrior	3
Gold Star	3	Welsh Black	3
Golden Arrow	3	Welsh Gold	3

Source: *Good Beer Guide 2016*.

Some British Beer Statistics

British breweries contribute hugely to the UK economy, as shown below.

Employees	870,000
Tax Revenues Generated	£13 billion
Wages/Salaries Paid	£10 billion

Source: *A Healthy Perspective on Beer* (British Beer & Pub Association, 2016).

UK Beer Weeks

Following a trend started in the USA, a number of British towns and cities now host week-long (or even longer) celebrations of beer, working with local pubs and breweries to stage a variety of beer-related events, from festivals, meet-the-brewer evenings and ale-trails to beer dinners, talks and tutored tastings. There are also a couple of national celebrations. The dates vary from year to year, and may straddle more than one month.

Month	Town/City
February	London
March	Sheffield
May	Norwich*
June	Manchester
July	Nottingham
August	Bristol
	London[†]
September	National Cask Ale Week
	Cheltenham
	Leeds
October	British Pub Week

* Norwich City of Ale   † London Beer City

The National Flavours of Hops

'English flavour is like a chamber orchestra, the hops giving simultaneously the high notes and the bass notes. In comparison, a Czech beer is more like a full orchestra with much more breadth to the sound, and an American hop gives more of a dance band with more emphasis on volume and brass. The recent New Zealand hops (e.g. Nelson Sauvin) are like adding a voice to the instrumental music.'

Dr Peter Darby, Wye Hops

A Beer Writers' Dinner

*Prepared by Andrew Bennett of the Park Lane Hotel, London,
for the Annual Dinner of the British Guild of Beer Writers 2015*

Fillet of Meagre Bass, Spiced Red Lentils, Spinach and Lime Sauce

or

English Golden Cross Goats' Cheese Tart, Textures of Beetroot,
Tarragon Dressing
served with
Brew By Numbers 01 Saison Citra, 5.5%

***

Cannelloni of Braised Denham Estate Venison Shoulder, Coffee
Marinated Loin, Cassoulet of White Beans and Pancetta
served with
Meantime Chocolate Porter, 6.5%

or

Cannelloni of Butternut Squash and Spinach, Coffee Marinated Tofu,
Cassoulet of White Beans and Heirloom Carrots
served with
Hook Norton Lion, 4%

***

Gingerbread & Bramley Apple Pudding with Crème Fraiche Anglaise
served with
Robinsons Old Tom Ginger, 8.5%

***

Cheese Platter: Norbury blue cheese, Peter Yard biscuits, honey
served with
Camden Town Brewery IHL, 6.2%

Famous Beers/Brands and Their Countries of Origin

Achel	Belgium	Coors	USA
Achouffe	Belgium	Corona	Mexico
Affligem	Belgium	Cruzcampo	Spain
Alhambra	Spain	Cusqueña	Peru
Amstel	Netherlands	DAB	Germany
Anchor Steam	USA	De Koninck	Belgium
Andechs	Germany	De Molen	Netherlands
Asahi	Japan	Delirium Tremens	Belgium
Augustiner	Germany	Dos Equis	Mexico
Baladin	Italy	Duvel	Belgium
Baltika	Russia	Efes	Turkey
Bavaria	Netherlands	Erdinger	Germany
Beamish	Ireland	Estrella Damm	Spain
Beck's	Germany	Farsons	Malta
Belle-Vue	Belgium	Faxe	Denmark
Bernard	Czech Republic	Fischer	France
Bintang	Indonesia	Flying Dog	USA
Bitburger	Germany	Foster's	Australia
Blue Moon	USA	Franziskaner	Germany
Boag's	Australia	Fürstenberg	Germany
Boon	Belgium	Goose Island	USA
Brahma	Brazil	Grimbergen	Belgium
Brooklyn	USA	Grolsch	Netherlands
Budweiser	USA	Guinness	Ireland
Budweiser Budvar	Czech Republic	Harp	Ireland
Cantillon	Belgium	Heineken	Netherlands
Carib	Trinidad	Hitachino Nest	Japan
Carling	Canada	Hoegaarden	Belgium
Carlsberg	Denmark	Holsten	Germany
Castle	South Africa	Hürlimann	Switzerland
Castlemaine XXXX	Australia	Jenlain	France
Ceres	Denmark	Jever	Germany
Ch'ti	France	Jupiler	Belgium
Chang	Thailand	Kaltenberg	Germany
Chimay	Belgium	Kanterbräu	France
Cisk	Malta	Keo	Cyprus
Coopers	Australia	Kingfisher	India

Kirin	Japan	Quilmes	Argentina
Krombacher	Germany	Red Stripe	Jamaica
Kronenbourg	France	Ringnes	Norway
Krusovice	Czech Republic	Rochefort	Belgium
Kwak	Belgium	Rodenbach	Belgium
La Trappe	Netherlands	Rolling Rock	USA
Labatt's	Canada	Sagres	Portugal
Lapin Kulta	Finland	St Bernardus	Belgium
Leffe	Belgium	Samichlaus.. Austria (was Switzerland)
Liefmans	Belgium	Samuel Adams	USA
Lindemans	Belgium	San Miguel	Phillippines/Spain
Little Creatures	Australia	Sapporo	Japan
Lion Stout	Sri Lanka	Schlenkerla	Germany
Löwenbräu	Germany	Schneider	Germany
Maes Pils	Belgium	Schöfferhofer	Germany
Mahou	Spain	Sierra Nevada	USA
Maisel's	Germany	Sinebrychoff	Finland
Menabrea	Italy	Singha	Thailand
Michelob	USA	Sol	Mexico
Mikkeller	Denmark	Spaten	Germany
Miller	USA	Staropramen	Czech Republic
Modelo	Mexico	Steinlager	New Zealand
Molson	Canada	Stella Artois	Belgium
Moosehead	Canada	Super Bock	Portugal
Moretti	Italy	Svyturys	Lithuania
Mort Subite	Belgium	Tiger	Singapore
Murphy's	Ireland	Timmermans	Belgium
Nils Oscar	Sweden	Toohey's	Australia
Nøgne Ø	Norway	Trois Monts	France
Okocim	Poland	Tsingtao	China
Oranjeboom	Netherlands	Tuborg	Denmark
Orval	Belgium	Vedett	Belgium
Pabst	USA	Veltins	Germany
Palm	Belgium	Victoria Beer	Australia
Paulaner	Germany	Warsteiner	Germany
Pelforth	France	Weihenstephan	Germany
Peroni	Italy	Westmalle	Belgium
Pilsner Urquell	Czech Republic	Westvleteren	Belgium
Pripps	Sweden	Zywiec	Poland

Ever Played the Lagerphone?

Proof that the worlds of beer and music go hand in hand comes in the form of the lagerphone, a home-made percussion instrument beloved of folk musicians, skifflers and morris dancers. Also known as a monkey stick, a mendoza or even to Australians as a Murrumbidgee river rattler, the lagerphone is a broom handle with a collection of beer bottle caps loosely attached. When the stick is tapped on the ground, the bottle caps jingle.

Where Are All the Hops Grown?

So how much farmland is given over to hop cultivation around the world?

Country	Hectares	Country	Hectares
USA	19,765	New Zealand	388
Germany	18,478	Ukraine	369
Czech Republic	4,700	Turkey	350
China	2,508	Romania	250
Poland	1,500	Austria	249
Slovenia	1,480	Russia	218
UK	1,000	Argentina	195
Spain	534	Japan	154
Australia	488	Belgium	148
France	440	Slovakia	140
South Africa	402	Bulgaria	18

Rest of the World.............. 374

Figures relate to 2016. Source: Hopsteiner/International Hop Growers' Convention.

Soccer Brew

Ethiopia is the country to visit if you fancy watching a beer-football derby. You can choose to support Harar Beer Bottling FC, which has links to a brewery in the city of Harar (the brewery was acquired from the Ethiopian government in 2011 by Heineken) or go for its rival, Dashan Beer – also known as Dashen Birra – which has associations with a brewery in Gondar.

Brewery Revivals

Rather than adopt a fresh name, a number of newly-established British breweries have set out to revive the name of a brewery that closed some years – if not decades – earlier. Here are some examples of such revivals.

Name	Location	Original Closure	Re-established
Brampton	Chesterfield	1955	2007
Hammerton	London	1950s	2014
Hercules	Belfast	1855	2014
Hurst	Hurstpierpoint	1910s	2012
Ilkley	Ilkley	1923	2009
Joule's	Market Drayton*	1974	2010
Kirkstall	Leeds	1983	2011
Lacons	Great Yarmouth	1968	2013
Lion†	Totnes	1926	2013
Lovibonds	Henley-on-Thames‡	1959	2005
Mauldons	Sudbury	1960	1981
Mordue	Wallsend	1879	1995
Nailsworth	Nailsworth	1908	2004
Nottingham	Nottingham	1952	2001
Phipps	Northampton	1974	2014
Rhymney	Blaenavon§	1978	2005
Truman's	London	1989	2010
Wrexham Lager	Wrexham	2000	2011

* Original location was Stone. † Revived as New Lion Brewery.

‡ Main brewery was at Greenwich. § Original location was Rhymney.

The Red Lioness

In 2011, Cathy Price popped into a Lake District pub to see how her horse was doing in the Grand National. The pub was called The Red Lion and a sign inside declared that this was the most common pub name in the UK. So began a long voyage of discovery as Cathy decided to visit all 656 pubs sharing that name. Five years later, mission completed, she related her adventures in a book, *The Red Lioness*. For her efforts, she was declared Beer Drinker of the Year 2016 by the All-Party Parliamentary Beer Group.

CAMRA's National Pubs of the Year

1988	Boar's Head, Kinmuck, Aberdeenshire
1989	Cap & Feathers, Tillingham, Essex
1990	Bell, Aldworth, Berkshire
1991	Great Western, Wolverhampton, West Midlands
1992	No award*
1993	Three Kings Inn, Hanley Castle, Worcestershire / Fisherman's Tavern, Broughty Ferry, Perth & Kinross
1994	Beamish Mary Inn, No Place, County Durham
1995	Coalbrookedale Inn, Coalbrookedale, Shropshire
1996	Halfway House, Pitney, Somerset
1997	Sair Inn, Linthwaite, West Yorkshire
1997/8	Volunteer Arms (Staggs), Musselburgh, Midlothian*
1998	Fat Cat, Norwich, Norfolk
1999	Rising Sun, Tipton, West Midlands
2000	Blisland Inn, Blisland, Cornwall
2001	Nursery, Heaton Norris, Greater Manchester
2002	Swan, Little Totham, Essex
2003	Crown & Thistle, Gravesend, Kent
2004	Fat Cat, Norwich, Norfolk
2005	Swan, Little Totham, Essex
2006	Tom Cobley Tavern, Spreyton, Devon
2007	Old Spot Inn, Dursley, Gloucestershire
2008	Kelham Island Tavern, Sheffield
2009	Kelham Island Tavern, Sheffield
2010	Harp, Covent Garden, London
2011	Bridge End Inn, Ruabon, Wrexham
2012	Baum, Rochdale, Greater Manchester
2013	Swan with Two Necks, Pendleton, Lancashire
2014	Salutation Inn, Ham, Gloucestershire
2015	Sandford Park Alehouse, Cheltenham, Gloucestershire

* Awards have been made at various times of the year, hence the peculiar dating.

Home-Brewing Now Legal Across the USA

Although home-brewing was federally legalized by US President Jimmy Carter in 1978, it took until 2013 for the last two American states – Alabama and Mississippi – to pass laws that permitted the practice across the USA. However, some states still place severe restrictions on home-brewing, including prohibiting home-brew from being taken out of the house in which it has been produced – a particular inconvenience for brewers who want to share and discuss the results of their labours with other practitioners or perhaps to take part in a home-brewing competition.

Some Important International Trade Fairs

Fair	Location	Month
Beer Attraction	Rimini, Italy	February
Beer X	Sheffield, UK	March
Bev Expo	Manchester, UK	June
Brau Beviale	Nuremberg, Germany	November
China Brew	Shanghai, China	October
Craft Brewers Conference/ BrewExpo America	Varies, USA	April
NBWA* Convention & Trade Show	Varies, USA	September
Pivovar	Moscow, Russia	October

* National Beer Wholesalers Association

Beer, the Great Job Creator

1 job in brewing generates:
> 1 job in agriculture
> 1 job in the supply chain
> 1 job in retail
> 18 jobs in pubs

Source: *The Beer Story: Facts on Tap 2016,* published jointly by the British Beer & Pub Association, CAMRA, SIBA and Hospitality Ulster.

National Maximum Permitted Blood Alcohol Levels for Driving in Europe

Grams/litre	Country
0.0	Czech Republic, Hungary, Romania, Slovakia
0.2	Cyprus, Estonia, Poland, Sweden
0.4	Lithuania
0.5	Austria, Belgium, Bulgaria, Croatia, Denmark, Finland, France, Germany, Greece, Ireland, Italy, Latvia, Luxembourg, Netherlands, Portugal, Slovenia, Spain, Switzerland
0.8	Malta, UK (0.5 in Scotland)

Different levels often apply for novice drivers and drivers of public transport.
Figures correct July 2016. Source: European Transport Safety Council.

How Pasteurisation Took a Hold

In 1866, the great Louis Pasteur published his *Etudes sur le vin*, a scientific study of wine which led him to extol the merits of heat-treatment in order to control fermentation and prevent wine going off. By around 1870, he had turned his attention to beer and was experimenting in Copenhagen before publishing his *Etudes sur la bière* in 1871. Pasteur found that, by heating beer to around 57°C (135°F) for a few minutes, he could prevent abnormal fermentation taking place. However, he may have been beaten to the punch as brewers and scientists in Germany and Austria, no doubt inspired by Pasteur's work with wine, had already begun to tamper with beer production. By the 1920s, the benefits of pasteurisation in cutting back bacterial infection had come to be widely recognised by bottling brewers. In 1923, for instance, Whitbread took over the smaller, but technologically more advanced, Forest Hill Brewery, largely to acquire its skill in bottling processed beers. As Whitbread took the techniques on board, 'Bright to the last drop' became a familiar slogan for the company's bottled beers. By December 1930, all but one of Whitbread's bottled beers (its celebrated Stout) were bright. Four or five decades before the cask ale crisis which saw the birth of CAMRA, real beer already had its back to the wall.

From the first edition of the *Good Bottled Beer Guide*, published in 1998.

The Railway Tap Revival

Some notable pubs and bars now in operation on British railway stations.

Station	Pub/Bar
Bridgnorth	Railwaymans Arms (Severn Valley Railway)
Bury Bolton Street	The Trackside (East Lancs Railway)
Carnforth	The Snug
Codsall	Codsall Station
Dewsbury	West Riding Refreshment Rooms
Harrogate	Harrogate Tap
Huddersfield	King's Head
	The Head of Steam
Kew	Tap on the Line
Kidderminster	King & Castle
London King's Cross	The Parcel Yard
London Paddington	The Mad Bishop & Bear
London St Pancras International	The Betjeman Arms
Manningtree	Manningtree Station Buffet
Newcastle upon Tyne	Centurion
Rawtenstall	Buffer Stops (East Lancs Railway)
Reading	The Three Guineas
Sheffield	The Sheffield Tap
Sowerby Bridge	Jubilee Refreshment Rooms
Stalybridge	Stalybridge Station Buffet
Urmston	The Steamhouse
Worksop	The Mallard
York	The York Tap

Rock Rumours

For years, speculation has been rife about how the band Blue Öyster Cult gained its name. One story doing the rounds was that a beer named Cully Stout Beer was the source, its letters rearranged to come up with the final product. Nice try but sadly no evidence can be found to show that such a beer ever existed.

Pints of Heavy

Ever lifted one of those thick, dimpled litre jugs of German beer? Pretty heavy, aren't they? So hats off to the amazing Oliver Struempfel, a waiter at the Gillemoos beer festival, held in the Bavarian town of Abensberg, who set an impressive world record in 2014 for carrying no fewer than 27 full jugs over a distance of 40 metres – and all without the help of a tray.

The World's Biggest Beer Brands

	Brand	% of world market
1	Snow	5.4
2	Tsingtao	2.8
3	Bud Lite	2.5
4	Budweiser	2.3
5	Skol	2.1
6	Yanjing	1.9
7	Heineken	1.5
8	Harbin	1.5
9	Brahma	1.5
10	Coors Light	1.3

Figures given are for 2015. Source: Euromonitor International.

The Beer Dress

In 2015, Australians Gary Cass and Donna Franklin, a scientist and a fashion designer, came together to create a dress made entirely from beer. The concept, admittedly, is hard to fathom but it revolves around adding acetobacter bacteria (sometimes used as a souring agent) to fermented beer. As the bacteria acts on the beer, cotton-like fibres of cellulose are created. Cass and Franklin harvested these fibres to create a new, odour-free material that they called nanollose, which could be grown and shaped into a seamless dress. They hope the breakthrough will change the way we produce and wear textiles. Who said beer wasn't a complex drink?

Fancy Becoming a Brewer?

Several international establishments offer educational and training courses in brewing. Below are the most prominent (note that varying degrees of brewing competence are addressed: courses are not just for beginners).

Country   *Establishment*
Australia   *Federation University*, Victoria federation.edu.au

Denmark   *Scandinavian School of Brewing*, Copenhagen
         brewingschool.dk

Germany   *Doemans Academy,* Munich doemans.org
         VLB, Berlin vlb-berlin.org
         Weihenstephan Technical University, Munich wzw.tum.de

UK   *Brew-School*, Bakewell brew-school.com
         Brewlab, University of Sunderland brewlab.co.uk
         Campden BRI, Nutfield campdenbri.co.uk
         International Centre for Brewing & Distilling,
         Heriot-Watt University, Edinburgh icbd.hw.ac.uk
         Institute of Brewing & Distilling, London ibd.org.uk
         Learn2Brew, Chelmsford learn2brew.co.uk
         PBC Brewery Installations, Bury
         pbcbreweryinstallations.com
         UBREW, London and Manchester ubrew.cc
         University of Nottingham pgstudy.nottingham.ac.uk

USA   *American Brewers Guild*, Salisbury, Vermont
         abgbrew.com
         Central Washington University, Ellensburg, Washington
         cwu.edu
         Cornell University, New York blogs.cornell.edu/brewing
         Master Brewers Association of the Americas, Madison,
         Wisconsin mbaa.com
         Siebel Institute of Technology, Chicago, Illinois
         siebelinstitute.com
         University of California – Davis, California
         universityextension.ucdavis.edu/brewing

Ale-pril Fools?

Strangely, some of the most bizarre beer news stories have emerged on the first day of April in recent years. Is this a coincidence? Perhaps not.

2009
Lovibonds Brewery takes the blame for traffic disruption in Henley-on-Thames, explaining that the roadworks causing problems are to install pipework that will carry Lovibonds beer to every household in the area.

2011
Lovibonds reveals it has accepted an offer of 1.4 million euros from Diageo for the rights to brew and distribute all of Lovibonds' brands, globally, with founder Jeff Rosenmeier taking on the role of chief beer officer in charge of innovation at Diageo.

2013
Brains unveils its own take on a classic Belgian beer style. The Cardiff brewery's Lamb-ic Ale, is a sour wheat beer fermented with wild yeasts and matured in casks with chops of the finest lamb from the hills of Ceredigion. Each pint will be served with a sprinkling of mint.

2014
Fuller's announces its has completed a beer pipeline, running from the brewery in Chiswick to the company's new London's Pride pub at Heathrow Terminal 2.

Greene King declares a pint-glass amnesty, urging customers to return any glasses that might somehow have made their way home with them over the years. The amnesty comes amid concerns that a shortage of sand could lead to restrictions on the manufacture of glass and pubs running out of drinking vessels.

Brains unveils plans for the first underwater pub. The new outlet, called the Aqua Nova, will sit five metres below sea level in Cardiff Bay and will be accessed by water taxi.

Timothy Taylor decides to boost its Tour de France-inspired beer, Le Champion, by adding frogs' legs for extra hoppiness.

Wood-ageing specialist Innis & Gunn declares that it is now to package its flagship beer, Original, in oak bottles. This will allow the beer to mature in the wood on the off-licence shelf. The bottle has been designed by company founder Dougal Sharp, using a lathe and instruction from YouTube.

America's Stone Brewing divulges details of its new helium beer. Stone Stochasticity Project Cr(He)am Ale is double dry-hopped and was inspired by experiments with nitro beers.

2015

Taking pity on man's best friend, who usually only gets a bowl of water when visiting a pub, Greene King introduces a new 'Doggy Menu', offering a variety of dishes approved by a team of canine tasters. On the menu are such treats as Chicken Liver Paw-te, Mixed Growl, Wagliatelle and Sticky Doggy Pudding.

Fuller's reveals that it has successfully managed to change its local London postcode from W4 to FST1, to reflect the initials of the brewery founders. Some streets have already altered signs to incorporate this.

Brains confirms the discovery of a natural ale spring in the Brecon Beacons. The source of the bubbling brown liquid, said to be dark mild, was stumbled upon by the brewery's packaging manager, Bev Ridge.

2016

Canadian company Cask, that somewhat confusingly specialises in canning, reveals details of an innovation that will change the way that bulk beer for parties will now be served. 'The Cag' is a giant aluminium can, three-feet high, that holds just over 13 gallons of beer. After use, the container can be simply crushed down and dropped into your recycling basket.

Florida's Coppertail Brewing unveils a new 5.9% ABV toothpaste, flavoured with its Free Dive IPA.

Bud on Bud

In 2015, AB InBev's Budweiser brewery in St Louis could hardly have had a more appropriate visitor. A 19-year-old man who was found on the site and arrested for trespass was revealed by police to be named Bud Weisser.

Varieties of Malting Barley

Here are some popular varieties of barley used for making beer in the UK.

Winter barley	*Spring barley*
(sown in the autumn)	*(sown in spring)*
Cassata	Concerto
Flagon	Golden Promise
Maris Otter	Optic
Pearl	Propino
Winsome	Publican
	Quench
	Tipple

Project William

Hats off, please, to Everards Brewery which has developed one of the most adventurous, and justly successful, models for running pubs. Some of Everards' houses are now part of the company's Project William scheme – launched in 2007 and named after brewery founder William Everard. The scheme sees Everards working closely with another, smaller brewery to acquire and then rejuvenate closed or struggling locals. Everards buys and refurbishes the property and the other brewery takes over the running of the pub, paying rent but having the right to sell its own beers and guests alongside at least one from Everards. This usually means a wide selection of beers from independent brewers are on sale, thus ensuring healthy trade for the pub and a good financial return for both Everards and the partner breweries, which include Ashover, Titanic and White Horse. Around 30 pubs have now benefited from this fresh, enlightened approach to beer retailing, some of which might now have been turned into private residences or even convenience stores had Everards not acted.

The Cheapest Cities for Beer

The places to head for on holiday if price is a factor in your choice of beer.

	City	Supermarket ($)	Bar ($)	Overall ($)
1	Bratislava, Slovakia	0.51	2.80	1.65
2	Kiev, Ukraine	0.69	2.63	1.66
3	Cape Town, South Africa	0.67	3.07	1.87
4	Krakow, Poland	0.82	2.92	1.87
5	Mexico City, Mexico	0.68	3.58	2.13
6	Belgrade, Serbia	0.44	3.95	2.19
7	Cairo, Egypt	1.01	3.76	2.39
8	Warsaw, Poland	0.87	4.02	2.45
9	Ljubljana, Slovenia	1.09	3.82	2.45
10	Budapest, Hungary	0.41	4.53	2.47

Selected Others:

	City	Supermarket ($)	Bar ($)	Overall ($)
15	Munich, Germany	0.61	4.61	2.61
23	Prague, Czech Republic	1.06	4.87	2.96
27	Edinburgh, UK	1.20	5.40	3.30
32	Brussels, Belgium	1.32	5.97	3.64
37	Dublin, Ireland	1.12	6.24	3.68
45	Manchester, UK	1.30	7.20	4.25
53	London, UK	1.20	8.22	4.71
58	Rome, Italy	0.88	9.14	5.01
62	New York, USA	1.49	9.22	5.36
64	Paris, France	0.75	10.08	5.41
65	Tokyo, Japan	2.30	8.66	5.48
66	Oslo, Norway	2.54	8.59	5.57
67	Zürich, Switzerland	1.35	10.03	5.69
68	Singapore, Singapore	2.16	9.33	5.75
69	Hong Kong, China	1.37	11.08	6.22
70	Lausanne, Switzerland	1.42	17.60	9.51

Figures show the average price, in US dollars (converted in April 2016), of a 33 cl bottle of major worldwide brands, plus one local brand, in supermarkets, and the average prices of 33 cl of local and imported draught beer in major hotel chain bars.

Source: Go Euro (travel search engine) 2016.

10 Great Beer Days Out

Tim Hampson – author of *CAMRA's 101 Beer Days Out* (CAMRA Books), a collection of wonderful suggestions for ways to explore the UK and enjoy some fine beers at the same time – selects ten of his favourite excursions.

1 Bermondsey Beer Mile
The Bermondsey beer mile is a fabulous insight into the vibrant world of London's hip craft beer scene. It's not a mile and won't be completed in under four minutes. Instead it takes a reasonable amount of walking and takes the best part of a drinking day, providing an unpolished, joyful and marvellously informal tour of some of the capital's brightest brewing stars.

2 Green Hop Beer Festival
On the second weekend of October, one of the country's brew pubs holds a festival of beers made with new-season hops. Nestling in the beautiful Teme Valley, near Worcester, the 14th-century Talbot at Knightwick, offers a feast of beers made with unkilned hops. The aromatics in fresh hops are delicate, and lack the intensity of a dried hop, but it's still possible to perceive hints of citrus, grass and the joy of a freshly-harvested crop.

3 Norwich City of Ale
Just a generation ago, in the era of mass-produced keg beer, Norfolk was a beer desert. Today it is in the vanguard of a beer revolution, hosting an annual ten-day festival in spring known as Norwich City of Ale – a city-wide celebration of real ale from local breweries.

4 Abergavenny Food Festival
For one weekend in September, Abergavenny hosts one of the UK's best known food and drink festivals, an event described as the Glastonbury of food fairs. It is a vibrant celebration that seems to take over every pore and crumb of the town, and beer features highly, too, with plenty of local ales on offer and the odd beer talk to tell you more about them.

5 Ascot Racecourse Beer Festival
The Ascot Racecourse Beer Festival is held over a Friday and Saturday every October. At least 200 thoroughbred real ales, ciders and perries are available and if anyone does tire of the beers then there is plenty of cracking, high quality racing taking place too.

6 Beamish Open Air Museum

Queen Victoria is no longer on the throne. World War I has yet to cast its dark shadow. The year is 1913, and the Sun Inn, like the rest of Beamish Open Air Museum, is frozen in history, a living example of when the North East was at the peak of its industrial pomp. The pub was rebuilt for the museum, lock stock, spittoon and barrel, from its original home in Bishop Auckland, County Durham, where it was known as the Tiger Inn. The small two-bar boozer has a tiny posh lounge with linoleum and leather seats – a wonderful retreat after taking in the historic exhibits.

7 Bog-Snorkelling in Mid-Wales

You don't have to be mad to live in Llanwrtyd Wells, but it seems to help. A veritable Olympics of alternative sports and beer festivals are organised in the town each year, including a man-versus-horse marathon, real ale wobbles on mountain bikes and a variety of bog-snorkelling disciplines such as the World Mountain Bike Bog Snorkelling championship. The Neuadd Arms Hotel's Bells bar features a display of winning boards for some of the town's more unusual championships.

8 The Bluebell Railway

The Bluebell Railway is now the only all-steam, standard-gauge railway in the country. On several evenings throughout the year the volunteers who run the line through the Sussex countryside also offer jazz-and-real ale events, the jazz playing at Horsted Keynes station.

9 CAMRA Founders' Walk

Chester may be renowned for its fine timber-framed buildings and two-mile ancient city wall but one night four young men went on a pub crawl there and changed the face of Britain's brewing industry. It was in March 1971 that the four founders of CAMRA – Bill Mellor, Graham Lees, Jim Makin and Michael Hardman – traipsed from Chester pub to Chester pub, along the way developing a consensus that the quality of much of the beer they had drunk was lousy. Thanks to their efforts in forming CAMRA, the beer in Chester is a lot better today.

10 Scottish Real Ale Festival

Edinburgh is the location for CAMRA's three-day extravaganza each June, celebrating the thriving brewing scene in Scotland, bringing together under one roof lipsmacking brews from most of the country's brewers.

The Top 20 Take-Home Beer Brands in the UK

	Brand	Hectolitres
1	Foster's	2,562,157*
2	Stella Artois	2,342,118
3	Carling	1,957,830
4	Budweiser	1,472,696
5	Carlsberg	1,373,620
6	Kronenbourg 1664	549,292
7	John Smith's	416,328
8	San Miguel	405,767
9	Guinness	405,103
10	Tennent's	381,157
11	Coors	372,993
12	Beck's	368,574
13	Corona	347,109
14	Peroni	287,194
15	Heineken	256,829
16	Old Speckled Hen	190,284
17	Cobra	140,624
18	Holsten	126,757
19	Skol	119,935
20	Tyskie	111,122

* Equivalent to 450,876,599 pints.

Figures, by volume to nearest hectolitre, correct to May 2016. Source: Nielsen ScanTrack.

Beer Day Britain

Britain now has its own national beer day – 15 June. This date was chosen because it was on that day of the year that the Magna Carta was sealed in 1215 with, as part of its provisions, the guarantee that there would be a single measure for ale across the kingdom, thereby protecting customers from swindlers and recognising the importance of beer to the country. Driven by beer educator Jane Peyton, Beer Day Britain was pioneered in 2015 and is now supported right across the industry. It is a day when Britain's beer-lovers are inspired to raise the profile of beer and take part in various beery events to celebrate the country's national alcoholic drink.

Beer Braised Pork Belly with a Creole Seasoning

Sean Paxton, one of America's leading exponents of beer cuisine, presents this recipe in *The Beer and Food Companion*, by Stephen Beaumont (Jacqui Small Publishing). Measurements allow for 18 x 100g (4oz) tasting menu portions but the recipe can also be used for stand-alone main courses.

Ingredients

1l (36 fl oz) bitter or mild ale (not hoppy, Sean uses Firestone Walker DBA)

1 tbsp brown sugar   1 tbsp sea salt

2 tsp thyme, fresh   2 bay leaves

1–4 tbsp Cajun spice blend, depending on heat level

2.2 kg (5 lb) pork belly, skin removed

Method

1 Pre-heat oven to 130°C/250°F/gas mark ½. In a pan just large enough to hold the belly – 22 x 33 cm (9 x 13 inches) should work – combine all ingredients except the belly and Cajun spice and mix well.

2 Add the pork belly, cover with foil and place in the centre of the oven and braise for four–six hours, until it is tender but not falling apart.

3 Once cooked, allow the pork belly to cool in the braising liquid. To flatten it out and make it easier to manage, cover the pork and liquid with cling film and place a smaller flat pan on top, weighing it down with canned food. Leave in refrigerator overnight.

4 The next day, remove the pork from the braising liquid and cut into pieces 2.5 cm (1 inch) square for a starter or 5 x 7.5 cm (2 x 3 inches) for a main course. Heat a cast-iron frying pan on a high heat. Sprinkle the pork with Cajun spice and press down.

5 Add a few tablespoons of butter to the pan, let it melt and, using tongs, place the pork belly seasoned side down. Cook for one–two minutes, searing and blackening the spices. Use your extractor fan as the meat will smoke.

6 Turn each of the pieces over and let them warm through. Remove from the pan and serve immediately.

Recommended Beer

Which beer you choose to drink with this will obviously depend on how spicy you make it, but for a mellow heat try a dunkel or a best bitter. For something more spicy, look for a hoppy hefeweizen, or hopfenweisse.

UK Breweries Still Using Dray Horses for Deliveries

In the days before motorised transport, horses were a familiar sight in towns, pulling the drays that delivered beer to pubs. Now just a trio of breweries maintain a team of these environmentally-friendly gentle giants for regular deliveries – not because they are economical, but because the public relations message is important, emphasising traditional standards.

Hook Norton   Samuel Smith   Wadworth

* Harveys also uses horses for some local deliveries, although these are hired in from an outside contractor.

A Brewery Rose Beneath the Nose

Brewery magnate Carl Jacobsen, son of Carlsberg founder JC Jacobsen, was a great patron of the arts but, in later life, he became somewhat eccentric. Every morning, his gardener was required to deliver one dark red rose which Carl would then clutch between his teeth for the rest of the day, believing the flower's fragrance would enhance the beauty of his life.

The Price of Your Pint

The table below highlights beer price increases in the UK versus those of other daily commodities since the time CAMRA was founded in 1971.

Item	1971 Price	2015 Price	% Increase
Pint of Milk	5p	45p	900%
Pound of Rump Steak	60p	605p	1008%
Sliced Loaf	9.5p	100p	1052%
Pint of Beer	12p	346p*	2883%

* Source: the *Good Pub Guide 2016* (Ebury Press).

Capital Beer: Amsterdam

For great beer in the Dutch capital don't miss these five excellent venues.

Arendsnest, Herengracht 90, 1015 BS
The focus is on Dutch beers in this rather genteel, wood-panelled, canalside bar, away from the tourist hubbub.

Beer Temple, Nieuwezijds Voorburgwal 250, 1012 RR
A rocking embassy for American craft beers, right in the heart of the city.

Café Gollem, Raamsteeg 4, 1012 VZ
The city's oldest specialist beer bar, a small, busy place that has generated a number of offspring branches.

De Prael, Oudezids Armsteeg 26, 1012 GP
Split-level brew pub located in the red-light district and providing work opportunities for folk recovering from mental illness and other difficulties.

In De Wildeman, Kolksteeg 3, 1012 PT
Unpretentious, two-roomed beer institution housed in a former distillery very close to Centraal station.

Gypsy Brewers

There are now numerous brewing companies that do not have their own breweries. Instead, they use spare capacity at other breweries to produce their beers. The dividing line between gypsy brewing (where the brewers are themselves hands-on) and contract brewing (where the beer is simply produced for them by another brewery) has become increasingly vague but here are some of the best-known claimants to the 'gypsy brewer' title.

Evil Twin (Denmark)
The Flying Dutchman (Finland)
Gypsy Inc (Denmark)
Local Option (US)
Mikkeller (Denmark)
Omnipollo (Sweden)
The Perfect Crime (US)
Pretty Things (US)
Ridgeway (UK)
ShinDigger (UK)
Stillwater (US)
To Øl (Denmark)

The Nitro-Keg Boom

During the 1990s, cask ale in the UK came under threat from new-fangled nitro-keg ales – filtered, pasteurised beers that were dispensed with a mixture of nitrogen and carbon dioxide gas that delivered a less prickly texture than using carbon dioxide gas alone. Drinkers were seduced by the glossy advertising that surrounded some of these beers and also by the 'theatre' of the pour, in which the beer swirled like milk before settling into a rather flat beer with a thick, creamy head. After the big national breweries scored a hit promoting these beers, some regional breweries followed suit, many simply naming their new creations 'Smooth' but others finding more adventurous names. Some of these beers still exist, but most have now been quietly forgotten by the breweries that survive.

Brewery	Nitro-keg Beer
Bass	Caffrey's/Worthington's Creamflow
Beamish	Red Ale
Brains	Dylan's
Brakspear	Supreme
Carlsberg-Tetley	Calder's Cream Ale
	Tetley Smooth Flow
Federation	Keoghan's Ale/Northumberland Smooth
Fuller's	London Cream
Gibbs Mew	Bridger's Gold
Greene King	Wexford's Irish Ale
Hall & Woodhouse	Dempsey's
Hardys & Hansons	Cool
Jennings	Cumberland Cream/Old Smoothy
Morrell's	Brewery Gate
Randalls	Sarnia Smooth
St Austell	Celtic Smooth/Cornish Cream
Scottish Courage	John Smith's Extra Smooth
Tennent's	Velvet Ale
Ushers	Milligan's Mist
Vaux	Lambton's
Whitbread	Boddingtons Gold

The Best Airport Bars

Each year, the Airport Food & Beverage Conference & Awards recognises the best airport terminal outlets around the world in a number of categories, including Airport Bar of the Year. Here are the winners to date.

2011	Center Bar, Zürich Airport
2012	Café Rembrandt, Amsterdam Airport
2013	Red Lion (Wetherspoon), Gatwick Airport
2014	Coopers Alehouse, Sydney Airport
2015	No awards made
2016	Windmill (Wetherspoon), Stansted Airport

Beer v Cider v Wine

UK drinks consumption (in litres) per head of total population, per year.

	Beer	*Cider*	*Wine*
1970	103.0	2.6	3.7
1980	118.3	4.0	8.1
1990	113.9	6.4	12.5
2000	88.4	10.2	17.2
2010	68.5	14.8	21.2
2014	67.7	12.3	20.2

Source: *British Beer & Pub Association Statistical Handbook 2015*.

US Craft Brewing Goes Right to the Top

In 2012, as beer fever continued to sweep across America, it was revealed that home-brewing was once again taking place at the official residence of the President of the USA. A short YouTube film was released, showing the production process, explaining how the beer was being made in small batches in the White House kitchen by chefs and then aged for four weeks in the cellars before being bottled and labelled by hand. Futhermore, all three of the beers created – Honey Ale, Honey Brown and Honey Porter – incorporated honey produced by the official White House beekeeper.

The Beer Fountain

In 2016, the Slovenian community of Zalec boldly voted to install a public beer fountain at a cost of around £133,000. The move was designed to draw attention to the town's hop-growing heritage and to attract more tourists to the area. The fountain will dispense a selection of local beers for a fee of six euros (three 30cl helpings, served in a commemorative mug).

Some UK Beer and Pub Trade Associations

ALMR (almr.org.uk)
The Association of Licensed Multiple Retailers, the national organisation representing the interests of UK pub and bar groups.

BBPA (beerandpub.com)
The British Beer & Pub Association, the trade body for the general UK brewing and pub industry, representing the biggest players in the field.

BII (bii.org)
The British Institute of Innkeeping, a body dedicated to raising professional standards in the British licensed retail industry via a series of courses and qualifications.

BFBI (bfbi.org.uk)
The Brewing, Food & Beverage Industry Suppliers Association, a body representing the supply chain from ingredients to packaging and beyond.

The Brewers' Company (brewershall.co.uk)
Historic livery company now actively involved in promoting and supporting the industry and in brewing education.

British Hop Association (britishhops.org.uk)
Formed by UK hop growers to co-ordinate their activities, including research and development, and to represent their interests politically.

Cask Marque (cask-marque.co.uk)
An industry-funded quality control organisation dedicated to improving the standard of beer service in pubs and bars.

Federation of Licensed Victuallers' Associations (flva.co.uk)
This organisation represents self-employed licensees in the UK, offering legal and other business advice.

The Hop Merchants Association
A body to represent companies that market and sell hops in the UK.

IBD (ibd.org.uk)
The Institute of Brewing & Distilling, an international body that offers training and qualifications for professional brewers and distillers.

IFBB (familybrewers.co.uk)
The Independent Family Brewers of Britain, an association of some of the UK's longest established breweries, all of which have family members still involved in the business.

The Maltsters' Association of Great Britain (ukmalt.com)
The representative body of UK malt producers.

SIBA (siba.co.uk)
The Society of Independent Brewers, the trade body for the smallest brewers in the UK, although some members are now major businesses.

Getting the Needle

There was a time when Americans got their fixes through a needle. We're not talking narcotics here: this is a tale about beer and it takes us back to the bleak days of Prohibition in the 1920s and early 1930s. In that sorry era, it was illegal to brew and/or sell alcoholic drinks in the USA, but brewers were allowed to produce what was laughingly called 'near beer' – a flimsy, cereal beverage with a tiny amount of alcohol in it (maximum 0.5% ABV). It was also possible to distil pure alcohol for industrial and medicinal purposes and it didn't take long for racketeers to come up with a way of putting the two together. To inject the alcohol into kegs of near beer, these devious fellows used large syringes that could slip through the cork bungs. Despite its illegality, 'needle beer' became well known, but what the resultant liquid must have tasted like one can only wonder. Not surprisingly, this dubious practice ceased once Prohibition was rescinded.

Beers' Dates of Birth

The following list reveals when some famous beers were first produced.

Adnams Broadside 1972

Adnams Southwold Bitter 1967

Alaskan Smoked Porter 1988

Anchor Liberty Ale 1975

Anchor Old Foghorn 1975

Batemans Victory Ale 1987

Batemans XXXB 1978

Brains SA 1958

Brains SA Gold 2006

BrewDog Punk IPA 2007

Brooklyn Lager 1988

Budweiser 1876

Budweiser Budvar 1895

Caledonian Deuchars IPA 1991

Carlsberg Special Brew 1950

Chimay Blue 1948

Chimay Red 1862

Chimay Triple 1966

Coopers Extra Strong
  Vintage Ale 1998

Double Maxim 1901

Efes 1969

Eggenberg Samichlaus 1979

Exmoor Gold 1986

Fuller's ESB 1971

Fuller's London Pride 1959

Fuller's Vintage Ale 1997

Gale's HSB 1959

Harveys Armada Ale 1988

Harveys Sussex Best Bitter 1955

Hoegaarden 1966

Hook Norton Old Hooky 1977

Hop Back Summer
  Lightning 1988

Innis & Gunn Oak Aged Beer ... 2003

Jenlain Ambrée 1922

Kronenbourg 1664 1952

Lees Harvest Ale 1986

Manns Brown Ale 1902

Marston's Old Empire 2003

Marston's Pedigree 1952

Meantime India Pale Ale 2005

Morland Old Speckled Hen ... 1979

Newcastle Brown Ale 1927

Palmers Tally Ho! 1949

Pilsner Urquell 1842

Ringwood Old Thumper 1979

Robinsons Old Tom 1899

St Bernardus Tripel 1992

Samuel Adams Boston Lager .. 1985

Schneider Aventinus 1907

Schneider Weisse 1872

Sharp's Doom Bar 1995

Shepherd Neame 1698 1998

Shepherd Neame Bishops
  Finger 1958

Shepherd Neame Spitfire 1990

Sierra Nevada
  Celebration Ale 1981

Sierra Nevada Pale Ale 1980

St Austell Tribute 1999

Stella Artois 1926

Taylor Landlord 1953

Thornbridge Jaipur 2005

Wadworth 6X 1923

Westmalle Dubbel 1926

Westmalle Tripel 1934

Woodforde's Wherry 1981

Young's Double Chocolate
  Stout 1997

The Most Popular UK Hops

The major hop varieties grown today in the UK, by the area cultivated.

Variety	Hectares	Variety	Hectares
Golding	123.98	Northdown	15.56
First Gold	99.56	Cascade	8.24
East Kent Golding	97.51	Boadicea	7.44
Fuggle	83.52	Pioneer	5.12
Target	79.99	Pilot	4.4
Pilgrim	68.44	Jester	4.32
Progress	59.83	Endeavour	4.0
Sovereign	55.78	Organic First Gold	2.0
Challenger	52.94	Olicana	1.62
Bramling Cross	46.07	Chinook	1.6
WGV	33.97	Organic Target	1.36
Admiral	29.91	Bullion	1.3

Other varieties 6.22

Figures relate to 2015. Source: Hopsteiner/International Hop Growers' Convention.

Cop the Boat Race

Anyone who drinks a lot of canned beer may wish to put their empties to good use by entering the Beer Can Regatta – although they'll have to fly to Australia to do so. This hugely popular charity event is held annually at Mindil Beach, Darwin, and run by the local Lions clubs. It began in 1974 and is now a popular family festival, staged each July and attracting around 15,000 spectators. Boats of all kinds can enter the race, as long as they have been created out of used beer cans, which are taped end to end and held together with chicken wire. Some designs are impressive and ingenious, incorporating thousands of empties and travelling sweetly over the water. At one time outboard motors were permitted but these have been banned since the 1980s when brewers began introducing aluminium cans, which buckle at a lower pressure. The aim of the race is to locate sunken treasure and return it to the shore. But piracy is rife, with water pistols and flour bombs used to distract the leaders and steal the prize.

All About the World's Favourite Hops

Hop	Country	Alpha Acid*	Typical Uses
Admiral	UK	14.8	British ales
Ahtanum	US	5.7	American ales
Amarillo	US	8.5	American ales
Apollo	US	17.0	American ales
Aurora	Slovenia	8.2	American/British ales
Boadicea	UK	8.5	British ales
Bobek	Slovenia	5.2	American/British ales
Bramling Cross	UK	6.9	British ales
Bravo	US	15.5	American ales
Brewer's Gold	Germany/US	9.0	German lagers
Bullion	UK	8.0	British ales
Cascade	US	5.5	American ales
Celeia	Slovenia	5.2	British ales
Centennial	US	10.5	American ales
Challenger	UK	7.5	British ales
Chinook	US	13.0	American ales
Citra	US	12.0	American ales
Cluster	US	7.0	American ales
Columbus	US	15.0	American ales
Crystal	US	4.5	American ales
El Dorado	US	15.0	American ales
Endeavour	UK	9.0	British ales
First Gold	UK	7.0	British ales
Fuggle	UK	4.5	British ales
Galaxy	Australia	13.5	American/British ales
Galena	US	13.0	American ales
Glacier	US	5.5	American ales
Golding	UK	5.5	British ales
Green Bullet	New Zealand	12.5	NZ ales
Hallertauer Hersbrucker	Germany	4.5	German lagers
Hallertauer Magnum	Germany	13.5	German lagers
Hallertauer Mittelfrüh	Germany	4.5	German lagers
Hallertauer Taurus	Germany	14.5	German lagers
Hallertauer Tradition	Germany	5.5	German lagers
Herkules	Germany	14.5	German lagers
Jester	UK	8.0	British ales

Liberty	US	4.0	American lagers
Marynka	Poland	9.0	Lagers
Mosaic	US	12.5	American ales
Motueka	New Zealand	7.5	NZ ales
Mount Hood	US	6.0	American lagers
Nelson Sauvin	New Zealand	12.5	NZ ales
Northdown	UK	8.0	British ales
Northern Brewer	UK/US	8.0	American/British ales
Nugget	US	13.0	American ales
Olicana	UK	7.5	British ales
Pacific Gem	New Zealand	15.0	NZ ales
Perle	US/Germany	8.0	German lagers
Pioneer	UK	9.0	British ales
Pilot	UK	9.5	British ales
Pride of Ringwood	Australia	10.0	Australian lagers
Progress	UK	6.5	British ales
Saaz	Czech Republic	3.5	Pilsners
Saphir	Germany	3.0	German lagers
Savinjski Golding	Slovenia	5.0	British ales
Simcoe	US	13.0	American ales
Sorachi Ace	US	13.0	American ales
Sovereign	UK	5.5	British ales
Spalt	Germany	4.0	German lagers
Sterling	US	7.5	British ales
Strisselspalt	France	2.0	French lagers
Summit	US	16.0	American ales
Super Galena	US	14.5	American ales
Target	UK	11.0	British ales
Tettnanger	Germany	4.5	German lagers
Tomahawk	US	16.0	American ales
Ultra	US	3.0	American ales
Warrior	US	16.5	American ales
Whitbread Golding Variety (WGV)	UK	6.5	British ales
Willamette	US	5.0	American ales
Zeus	US	14.5	American ales

* Alpha acid content, which is an indicator of the bitterness of the hop, varies from crop to crop. The figures given are approximations of general alpha content.

The Best US Cities for Beer-Lovers

Thinking of moving to the USA? Check out this list of the best beer cities before making any decisions. The ranking takes into account the number of breweries in the state per 100,000 adults aged 21+; the number of active brewery permits in each state; state beer taxes; the median home sale price; and the city's 'walk score' (discouraging drinking and driving).

1   Pittsburgh, Pennsylvania
2   Buffalo, New York
3   Milwaukee, Wisconsin
4   Grand Rapids, Michigan
5   Philadelphia, PA
6   Portland, Oregon
7   Denver, Colorado
8   Detroit, Michigan
9   Cleveland, Ohio
10   St Louis, Missouri
11   Madison, Wisconsin
12   Long Island, New York
13   Seattle, Washington
14   Cincinnati, Ohio
15   San Francisco, California

Source: Redfin (real estate company) and the Beer Institute (US trade association), 2016.

Charles Wells Pubs in France

Bombardier, Paris
Charles Dickens, Bordeaux
Cross of St George, Paris
De Danu, Toulouse
Elephant & Castle, Lyon
English Country Kitchen, Bordeaux

George & Dragon, Toulouse
King Arthur, Lyon
London Town, Toulouse
Robin Hood, Montpellier
Shakespeare, Montpellier
Sherlock Holmes, Bordeaux
Starfish, Bordeaux

Heritage Pubs

The National Inventory of Historic Pub Interiors is a geographical list compiled by CAMRA's Pub Heritage Group. The product of more than 20 years of research, it identifies pubs that have intact traditional interiors or features/rooms of national importance that are deserving of protection.

England

Bedfordshire
Broom, Cock
Luton, Painters Arms

Berkshire
Aldworth, Bell

Buckinghamshire
West Wycombe, Swan

Cambridgeshire
Peterborough, Hand & Heart

Cheshire
Alpraham, Travellers Rest
Barthomley, White Lion
Gawsworth, Harrington Arms
Haslington, Hawk Inn
Macclesfield, Castle
Scholar Green, Bleeding Wolf

Cornwall
Falmouth, Seven Stars
Penzance, Admiral Benbow

Cumbria
Bassenthwaite Lake, Pheasant
Broughton Mills,
   Blacksmiths Arms

Derbyshire
Derby, Olde Dolphin Inne
Elton, Duke of York
Glossop, Crown Inn
Makeney, Holly Bush Inn
Spondon, Malt Shovel
Wardlow Mires, Three Stags Heads

Devon
Drewsteignton, Drewe Arms
Luppitt, Luppitt Inn
Topsham, Bridge Inn

Dorset
Pamphill, Vine
Worth Matravers,
   Square & Compass

Durham
Barningham, Milbank Arms
Durham, Victoria

Essex
Aveley, Old Ship
Mill Green, Viper

Gloucestershire & Bristol
Ampney St Peter, Red Lion
Bristol, Kings Head
Duntisbourne Abbots,
   Five Mile House (C)
Purton, Berkeley Arms

Hampshire
Southampton City Centre,
   Red Lion
Steep, Harrow

Herefordshire
Kington, Ye Olde Tavern
Leintwardine, Sun Inn
Leysters, Duke of York

Hertfordshire
Flaunden, Green Dragon
Trowley Bottom, Rose & Crown

Kent
Cowden Pound, Queens Arms
Ightham Common, Old House
Snargate, Red Lion (Doris's)

Lancashire
Goosnargh, Ye Horns Inn
Great Harwood, Victoria
Preston, Black Horse
St Annes on Sea, Burlingtons Bar
   (at the Town House)

Leicestershire
Whitwick, Three Horseshoes

Lincolnshire
Scunthorpe, Berkeley

Greater London
Barkingside, Doctor Johnson (C)
Bayswater, W2, Victoria
Bellingham, SE6, Fellowship Inn
Bermondsey, SE1, Lord Nelson
Blackfriars, EC4, Black Friar
Bloomsbury, WC1, Duke (of York)

Clapham Junction, SW11,
   Falcon
Covent Garden, WC2, Salisbury
Cranford, Queens Head
Crouch End, N8, Queens
Dagenham, Eastbrook
Fitzrovia, W1, Flying Horse
Fleet Street, EC4,
   Olde Cheshire Cheese
Hackney, E8, Dolphin
Hanwell, W7, Kings Arms
Harringay, N4, Salisbury
Harrow-on-the-Hill, Castle
Hatton Garden, EC1,
   Olde Mitre
Hayes, Angel
Herne Hill, SE24, Half Moon (C)
Highgate, N6, Winchester
Holborn, WC1, Cittie of Yorke
   Princess Louise
Kensington, W8, Windsor Castle
Kilburn, NW6, Black Lion
Maida Vale, W9, Prince Alfred
   Warrington
Marylebone, W1, Barley Mow
Notting Hill, W11, Elgin Arms
Ruislip, Woodman
Smithfield, EC1, Hand & Shears
   Viaduct Tavern
Soho, W1, Argyll Arms
   Dog & Duck
South Kenton, Windermere
Southwark, SE1, George Inn
St James's, SW1, Red Lion
St John's Wood, NW8,
   Crocker's Folly
Tooting, SW17, Kings Head
Upton Park, East Ham, E6,
   Boleyn

Wandsworth, SW18,
   Spread Eagle
West Brompton, SW10,
   Fox & Pheasant
West Ealing, W13, Forester

Greater Manchester
Altrincham, Railway
Brunswick, Mawson Hotel (C)
Bury, Old White Lion
Eccles, Lamb Hotel
   Royal Oak
Eccles, Patricroft, Stanley Arms
Eccles, Peel Green, Grapes
Farnworth, Shakespeare
Gorton, Plough
Heaton Norris, Nursery Inn
Heywood, Grapes
Manchester City Centre,
   Britons Protection
   Circus Tavern
   Hare & Hounds
   Marble Arch
   Mr Thomas Chop House
   Peveril of the Peak
Oldham Centre, Royal Oak
Rochdale, Cemetery Hotel
Salford, Coach & Horses
Stalybridge, Station Buffet
Stockport, Arden Arms
   Swan with Two Necks
Stockport, Edgeley, Alexandra
Westhoughton, White Lion
Wigan, Springfield, Springfield
Withington, Turnpike

Merseyside
Birkenhead, Crown
   Stork Hotel

Liscard, Primrose
Liverpool City Centre,
   Crown Hotel
   Lion Tavern
   Peter Kavanagh's
   Philharmonic Dining Rooms
   The Vines
Liverpool, Walton, Prince Arthur
Lydiate, Scotch Piper
Sutton Leach, Wheatsheaf
Waterloo,
   Volunteer Canteen

Norfolk
Kenninghall, Red Lion

Northumberland
Berwick-on-Tweed, Free Trade
Netherton, Star

Nottinghamshire
Arnold, Daybrook, Vale Hotel
Beeston, Crown
Nottingham City Centre,
   Olde Trip To Jerusalem
West Bridgford, Test Match Hotel

Oxfordshire
Steventon, North Star

Shropshire
Selattyn, Cross Keys
Shrewsbury, Loggerheads
Telford, Wrockwardine Wood,
   Bulls Head

Somerset
Bath, Old Green Tree
   Star Inn

Faulkland, Tuckers Grave Inn
Huish Episcopi, Rose & Crown
Witham Friary, Seymour Arms

Staffordshire
Audley, Butchers Arms
Burton upon Trent,
  Coopers Tavern
Cannock, Crystal Fountain
High Offley, Anchor Inn
Rugeley, Red Lion
Stoke-on-Trent, Hanley,
  Coachmakers Arms
Stoke-on-Trent, Pittshill (Tunstall),
  Vine

Suffolk
Brent Eleigh, Cock
Bury St Edmunds, Nutshell
Ipswich, Margaret Catchpole
Laxfield, Kings Head
Pin Mill, Butt & Oyster

Sussex (East)
Brighton, King & Queen
Hadlow Down, New Inn
Hastings, General Havelock

Sussex (West)
Balls Cross, Stag Inn
The Haven, Blue Ship

Tyne & Wear
Gateshead, Central
South Shields, Stags Head
Sunderland Centre, Dun Cow
Sunderland, Millfield,
  Mountain Daisy

West Midlands
Birmingham, Aston, Bartons Arms
Birmingham, Digbeth, Anchor
  White Swan
  Woodman
Birmingham, Erdington, Red Lion
Birmingham, Handsworth,
  Red Lion (C)
Birmingham, Hockley,
  Rose Villa Tavern
Birmingham, King's Heath,
  Hare & Hounds
Birmingham, Nechells,
  Villa Tavern
Birmingham, Northfield,
  Black Horse
Birmingham, Stirchley,
  British Oak
Bloxwich, Romping Cat
  Turf Tavern
Dudley, Shakespeare (C)
Netherton, Old Swan
Oldbury, Waggon & Horses
Rushall, Manor Arms
Sedgley, Beacon Hotel
Smethwick, Waterloo (C)
Upper Gornal, Britannia
Wednesbury, Horse & Jockey
Wednesfield, Vine

Wiltshire
Easton Royal, Bruce Arms
Salisbury, Haunch of Venison

Worcestershire
Bretforton, Fleece
Clent, Bell & Cross
Defford, Cider House
Hanley Castle, Three Kings

Worcester, Paul Pry
Worcester, Ronkswood, Punch Bowl

Yorkshire (East)
Beverley, White Horse (Nellie's)
Bridlington, Station Buffet
Hull, Olde Black Boy
   Olde White Harte
   Polar Bear
   White Hart Hotel

Yorkshire (North)
Beck Hole, Birch Hall Inn
Boroughbridge,
   Three Horse Shoes
Middlesbrough, Zetland
Selby, New Inn
York, Blue Bell
York, Bishophill, Golden Ball
York, Clementhorpe, Swan

Yorkshire (South)
Barnburgh, Coach & Horses
Doncaster, Plough
Sheffield City Centre, Bath Hotel
   Sheffield Tap

Yorkshire (West)
Bradford, New Beehive Inn
Halifax, Three Pigeons
Heath, Kings Arms
Leeds, Burley, Cardigan Arms
   Rising Sun (C)
Leeds City Centre,
   Whitelocks Ale House
Leeds, Hunslet, Garden Gate
Leeds, Leeds Bridge, Adelphi
Leeds, Lower Wortley, Beech
Norwood Green, Old White Beare

Northern Ireland
Belfast & Lisburn
Belfast City Centre, Crown Bar
Belfast, West, Fort Bar
Lisburn, Smithfield House

County Antrim
Ballycastle, Boyd Arms
   House of McDonnell
Ballyeaston, Carmichaels
Bushmills, Bush House

County Armagh
Camlough, Carraghers Bar
Portadown, Mandeville Arms

County Down
Killyleagh, Dufferin Arms

County Fermanagh
Enniskillen, Blakes of the Hollow
Irvinestown, Central Bar

County Londonderry
Limavady, Owens Bar

Scotland
Aberdeen & Grampian
Aberdeen, The Grill
Craigellachie, Fiddichside Inn

Borders
Tweedsmuir, Crook Inn (C)

Dundee & Tayside
Dundee, Clep Bar
   Frews Bar
   Speedwell Bar

Edinburgh & The Lothians
Edinburgh, Leith, Central Bar
Edinburgh, New Town,
   Abbotsford
   Barony Bar
   Café Royal
   HP Mather (Mathers Bar)
   Kenilworth
   Oxford Bar
Edinburgh, Newington,
   Leslie's Bar
Edinburgh, Tollcross, Bennets Bar
Prestonpans, Prestoungrange
   Gothenburg
West Calder, Railway Inn

Glasgow & West of Scotland
Glasgow City Centre,
   Horse Shoe Bar
   Laurieston Bar
   Old Toll Bar (C)
   Steps Bar
Glasgow, Govan, Brechins
Glasgow, Shettleston,
   Portland Arms
   Railway Tavern
Kilmelford, Cuilfail Hotel
Lochgilphead, The Comm
Paisley, Bull Inn
Renton, Central Bar

Highlands & Western Isles
Rosemarkie, Plough

Kingdom of Fife
Kincardine, Railway Tavern
Kirkcaldy, Feuars Arms
Leslie, Auld Hoose

Wales
Glamorgan
Cardiff City Centre,
   Golden Cross

Mid Wales
Cemmaes Road, Dovey Valley
   Hotel
Llanidloes, Crown & Anchor
Rhayader, Lion Royal Hotel

North-East Wales
Ysceifiog, Fox

North-West Wales
Bethesda, Douglas Arms
Conwy, Albion Ale House

West Wales
Court Henry, New Cross Inn
Pontfaen, Dyffryn Arms

Note: (C) indicates that the pub had been closed for a long time by August 2016.

The 20 Largest American Craft Breweries

	Brewery	US Barrels
1	DG Yuengling and Son, Inc.	2,805,367
2	Boston Beer Co	2,525,000
3	Sierra Nevada Brewing Co	1,222,369
4	New Belgium Brewing Co	914,063
5	Gambrinus	679,846
6	Lagunitas Brewing Co*	624,463
7	Bell's Brewery, Inc.	370,640
8	Deschutes Brewery	345,689
9	Minhas Craft Brewery	343,246
10	Stone Brewing Co	325,645
11	Ballast Point Brewing & Spirits*	277,152
12	Brooklyn Brewery	277,000
13	Firestone Walker Brewing Co	273,869
14	Oskar Blues Brewing Holding Co	261,000
15	Duvel Moortgat USA	245,000
16	Dogfish Head Craft Brewery	236,762
17	Matt Brewing Co	223,215
18	SweetWater Brewing Co	218,420
19	Harpoon Brewery	204,000
20	New Glarus Brewing Co	194,894

Figures given are for 2015. * Breweries since acquired by larger companies.

Source: Brewers Association. For the US definition of a craft brewer see page 14.

NCIS: Masham

In 2012, Masham brewery Theakston launched a new ale based on a beer created for a hit TV programme. The previous Christmas, unbeknown to the North Yorkshire brewers, characters in the US series *NCIS: Los Angeles* welcomed in the festive season by drinking from a wooden cask of imported Theakston's Christmas Ale, said to have been brewed since the days of Charles Dickens. At the time, the beer was purely fictitious. Theakston itself did not even have a Christmas Ale so it set about creating one after receiving enquiries about where the TV beer could be bought. The result was a 4.7% ABV beer that included both raisins and cinnamon.

Most people would never drink a whole bottle of White Shield

During its lifetime many traditions and methods have grown up around the pouring of White Shield. In fact, there is quite an art to pouring a White Shield.

And if you've never poured it before you might find it a bit tricky. But keep at it. Because, of course, after the first taste you're bound to want to keep practising.

1. The point to remember when pouring White Shield is to leave the last tablespoon of beer with the sediment in the bottom of the bottle.

2. Pour at eye level (you have to watch for that sediment), keeping the bottle and the glass almost horizontal. Then, without resting the bottle on the rim of the glass pour the beer along the glass very slowly.

3. Now gradually straighten the glass as it fills – but avoid any violent movement of the bottle which would disturb the sediment.

4. You should now have a beautifully clear glass of White Shield and a bottle with the sediment in. If you didn't pour it to your own satisfaction maybe a little homework is called for. But remember, it's your White Shield – never let anyone else pour it for you!

On the other hand...

There are two other schools of thought to the pouring of White Shield.

One is practised by the White Shield brewers. That is to pour the White Shield in the approved manner leaving the sediment in the bottle, drink the beer and then knock back the sediment at the end.

The other is also to pour White Shield in the approved manner, but then tip the natural sediment in and watch the goodness start to sink to the bottom.

Pouring a Bottle-Conditioned Beer

Because of the natural sediment (mostly comprising living, active yeast) that sometimes remains loose in the bottle, just a little care needs to be taken when pouring a bottle-conditioned beer, as the vintage advert opposite for one of Britain's most historic bottled beers, Worthington's White Shield, graphically explains. Just remember: practice makes perfect!

What's Your Tipple?

For every ten drinks sold in a pub:
1 is wine, 1 is cider, 1 is spirits, 7 are beers

Source: *The Beer Story: Facts on Tap 2016*, published jointly by the British Beer & Pub Association, CAMRA, SIBA and Hospitality Ulster.

It's Not All Pilsner, You Know

The Czech Republic may be the birthplace of the world's most copied beer style, but there are other forms of traditional beer available in the country. Here are a few words to help you navigate the Czech beer scene.

Výčepní	'Tap beer' (draught beer up to 11° Balling*)
Ležák	Literally 'lager' (but covering all beer styles between 11 and 13° Balling)
Speciál	Beers topping 13° Balling (usually strong lager and can be light or dark)
Světlý	A pale-coloured beer (golden in colour)
Polotmavý	A semi-dark-coloured beer (amber)
Tmavý	A dark-coloured beer (dark amber and deeper)
Černý	A black beer (at the darker end of tmavý)

* Balling is a scale measuring the amount of sugar in a beer before fermentation. A beer of 11° Balling usually turns out at around 4.5% ABV and 13° at just over 5%.

British Beer & Pub Association Members

The British Beer & Pub Association (BBPA) is a trade body representing brewing and retailing businesses that account for some 90% of all the beer brewed in the UK and own roughly half of all the country's pubs.

Admiral Taverns Ltd	Holden's Brewery Ltd
Adnams plc	Hook Norton Brewery Co Ltd
Anheuser-Busch InBev	Hydes Brewery Ltd
Arkell's Brewery Ltd	JC & RH Palmer Ltd
Black Sheep Brewery plc	JW Lees & Co
Brakspear Pub Company	Joseph Holt Ltd
Budweiser Budvar UK	Kingfisher Beer
Camerons Brewing Ltd	Liberation Group
Carlsberg UK	Maclay Group plc
Charles Wells Ltd	Marston's plc
Daleside Brewery	McMullen & Sons Ltd
Daniel Batham & Son Ltd	Miller Brands UK
Daniel Thwaites plc	Mitchells of Lancaster Ltd
Diageo plc	Molson-Coors Ltd
Elgood & Sons Ltd	Moorhouse's Brewery (Burnley) Ltd
Enterprise Inns plc	Punch Taverns
Everards Brewery Ltd	RW Randall
Felinfoel Brewery Co Ltd	Route Organisation
Frederic Robinson Ltd	SA Brain & Co Ltd
Fuller, Smith & Turner plc	Shepherd Neame Ltd
George Bateman & Son Ltd	St Austell Brewery Co Ltd
Gray & Sons (Chelmsford) Ltd	T&R Theakston
Hall & Woodhouse Ltd	Thomas Hardy Brewing & Packaging Ltd
Harvey & Son (Lewes) Ltd	Timothy Taylor & Co Ltd
Heavitree Brewery plc	Titanic Brewery
Heineken UK (London)	Wadworth & Co Ltd
Heron & Brearley Ltd	Weston Castle
Hogs Back Brewery Ltd	Young & Co's Brewery plc

Names of companies as listed by the BBPA in June 2016.

Who Makes the Most Beer?

Total beer production around the world, shown by country, by volume.

Country	Million hl	Country	Million hl
China	465.0	Angola	11.2
USA	225.8	Turkey	10.0
Brazil	133.0	Austria	9.1
Germany	96.0	Ireland	8.0
Mexico	82.5	Cameroon	7.9
Russia	70.1	Portugal	7.5
Japan	53.8	Chile	6.3
UK	41.5	Denmark	6.2
Poland	39.3	Hungary	6.2
Vietnam	38.2	Zaire	6.1
Spain	34.0	Cambodia	5.4
South Africa	31.7	Taiwan	5.3
Nigeria	27.1	Kenya	5.2
Netherlands	23.8	Ethiopia	5.2
Thailand	23.1	Bulgaria	4.7
Canada	22.6	Sweden	4.6
Colombia	22.2	Tanzania	4.4
Venezuela	21.5	Laos	4.3
South Korea	21.5	Finland	4.0
India	20.0	Greece	3.6
Czech Republic	19.7	Dominican Republic	3.6
France	18.9	Zambia	3.6
Ukraine	18.6	Switzerland	3.5
Belgium	18.0	Myanmar	3.5
Philippines	17.2	Uganda	3.5
Australia	17.1	Croatia	3.4
Romania	16.7	Lithuania	3.2
Argentina	16.5	Mozambique	3.0
Peru	13.6	Slovakia	2.9
Italy	13.1	New Zealand	2.9

Rest of the World 101.0

Figures relate to 2015. Source: Hopsteiner/International Hop Growers' Convention 2016.

How Many Units?

Safe drinking limits are commonly discussed in units of alcohol. In the UK, one unit is defined as 10 ml of pure alcohol. The following table shows approximately how many units are in pints of beer of varying strengths.

ABV	Units/pint	ABV	Units/pint
2.0%	1.136	6.5%	3.692
2.5%	1.42	7.0%	3.976
3.0%	1.704	7.5%	4.26
3.5%	1.988	8.0%	4.544
4.0%	2.272	8.5%	4.828
4.5%	2.556	9.0%	5.112
5.0%	2.84	9.5%	5.396
5.5%	3.124	10.0%	5.68
6.0%	3.408	10.5%	5.964

Note: The most recent UK Government advice is for both men and women not to regularly drink more than 14 units a week.

Major US Brewpub Chains

	Brewpub Chain	Outlets*
1	Gordon Biersch Brewery Restaurants	34
2	Granite City Brewing Co	34
3	Rock Bottom Restaurants	33
4	McMenamins Breweries	25
5	RAM/Big Horn Brewery	17
6	Iron Hill Brewery & Restaurant	11
7	Slesar Bros Brewing Co	6
8	Appalachian Brewing Co	6
9	Hofbrauhaus	5
10	Smoky Mountain Brewery	4

* Excludes non-brewing restaurants. Some outlets are operated under different names.
Figures given are for 2015. Source: Brewers Association.

CAMRA's Champion Beers of Britain

The Campaign for Real Ale's Champion Beer of Britain contest is judged on the first day of the Great British Beer Festival each summer. It is the UK's most prestigious cask ale competition, with all beers judged in categories, before an overall winner is elected. Here are the champions to date. Brewers' records in the competition can be found on pages 96–7 and 120.

1978	Thwaites Best Mild / Fuller's ESB	1997	Mordue Workie Ticket
1979	Fuller's London Pride	1998	Coniston Bluebird Bitter
1980	Thwaites Best Mild	1999	Taylor Landlord
1981	Fuller's ESB	2000	Moorhouse's Black Cat Mild
1982	Taylor Landlord	2001	Oakham JHB
1983	Taylor Landlord	2002	Caledonian Deuchars IPA
1984	No event	2003	Harvlestoun Bitter & Twisted
1985	Fuller's ESB	2004	Kelham Island Pale Rider
1986	Batemans XXXB	2005	Crouch Vale Brewers Gold
1987	Pitfield Dark Star	2006	Crouch Vale Brewers Gold
1988	Ringwood Old Thumper	2007	Hobsons Mild
1989	Fuller's Chiswick Bitter	2008	Triple fff Alton's Pride
1990	Ind Coope Burton Ale	2009	Rudgate Ruby Mild
1991	Mauldons Black Adder	2010	Castle Rock Harvest Pale
1992	Woodforde's Norfolk Nog	2011	Mighty Oak Oscar Wilde
1993	Adnams Extra	2012	Coniston No.9 Barley Wine
1994	Taylor Landlord	2013	Elland 1872 Porter
1995	Cottage Norman's Conquest	2014	Taylor Boltmaker
1996	Woodforde's Wherry	2015	Tiny Rebel Cwtch
		2016	Binghams Vanilla Stout

Bulk Delivery

As if to prove that things are bigger and better in Texas, in 2014 a local brewery pioneered an extra large box of beer. Forget about the humble six-pack, Austin Beerworks put together a special 99-pack of its Peacemaker Anytime Ale, limited supplies of which went on sale in local stores for the conveniently appropriate price of $99.99. Weighing nearly six stone (82 pounds), and stretching for more than seven feet, each pack contained three rows of 33 cans of beer. So stick that in your supermarket trolley!

Community-Owned Pubs

A list of British pubs that have been collectively purchased – in many cases saved from closure – by their customers and other locals and are now run as community ventures. Some of these are owned by local parish councils.

Angel, Spinkhill, Derbyshire
Angel Inn, Grosmont, Gwent
Anglers Rest, Bamford, Derbyshire
Antwerp Arms, Tottenham, London
Beauchamp Arms, Dymock, Gloucestershire*
Bell Inn, Bath, Somerset
Bevy, Brighton, East Sussex
Black Buoy, Wivenhoe, Essex
Bull, Great Milton, Oxfordshire
Butchers Arms, Crosby Ravensworth, Cumbria
Cadeleigh Arms, Cadeleigh, Devon
Case is Altered, Bentley, Suffolk
Cherry Tree Inn, Cherry Willingham, Lincolnshire
Crown, Clunton, Shropshire
Crown Inn, Dilwyn, Herefordshire
Cwmdu Inn, Cwmdu, Carmarthenshire
Dog Inn, Belthorn, Lancashire
Dolphin, Bishampton, Worcestershire
Farriers Arms, Mersham, Kent
Fleece Inn, Hillesley, Gloucestershire
Foresters Arms, Carlton-in-Coverdale, North Yorkshire
Fox & Goose, Hebdenbridge, West Yorkshire
Fox & Hounds, Charwelton, Northamptonshire
Fox & Hounds, Denmead, Hampshire
Fox & Hounds, Ennerdale Bridge, Cumbria
George & Dragon, Hudswell, North Yorkshire
Glan Llyn Inn, Clawddnewydd, Ruthin
Globe, Newcastle upon Tyne
Golden Ball, Bishophill, York
Green Man, Thriplow, Cambridgeshire
Green Man, Toppesfield, Essex
Heneage Arms, Hainton, Lincolnshire
Hollybush, Seighford, Staffordshire

Hope, Carshalton, London
Ivy House, Nunhead, London
Jolly Farmer, Cookham Dean, Berkshire
King's Arms, Shouldham, Norfolk
Maybush, Great Oakley, Essex
Merrie Lion, Fenny Compton, Warwickshire
New Inn, Manaccan, Cornwall
New Inn, Shipton Gorge, Dorset†
Old Crown, Hesket Newmarket, Cumbria
Olde Vic, Stockport, Greater Manchester
Pengwern, Llan Ffestiniog, Gwynedd
Pheasant, Neenton, Shropshire
Plough, Horbling, Lincolnshire*
Plough & Fleece, Horningsea, Cambridgeshire
Punch Bowl Inn, Battisford, Suffolk
Punch Bowl Inn, Great Broughton, Cumbria
Raven Inn, Llanarmon-y-Ial, Denbighshire†
Red Lion, Arlingham, Gloucestershire
Red Lion, Preston, Hertfordshire
Rose & Crown, Slaley, Northumberland
Royal Oak, Rushton Spencer, Staffordshire
Royal Oak Inn, Meavy, Devon*
Saith Seren, Wrexham
Seven Stars, Marsh Baldon, Oxfordshire
Sherlock Inn, Sherlock Row, Berkshire
Shuckburgh Arms, Southwick, Northamptonshire
Sorrel Horse, Shottisham, Suffolk
Star Inn, Salford, Greater Manchester
Stoke Canon Inn, Stoke Canon, Devon
Tafarn y Fic, Llithfaen, Gwynedd
Tally Ho, Hungerford Newton, Berkshire
Tally Ho, Littlehempston, Devon
Three Horseshoes, Thursley, Surrey
Tyn-Y-Capel, Minera, Wrexham
Village Swan, Ivinghoe Aston, Buckinghamshire
White Hart, Wolvercote, Oxfordshire
White Horse, Upton, Norfolk

* Owned by the parish council. † Leased by the community.

Capital Beer: Copenhagen

Five outstanding beer venues to head for while in Denmark's biggest city.

Black Swan, Borgergade 93, 1300
Small haven of quiet with 14 beer taps, just a short distance away from the bustle of the city.

Fermentoren, Halmtorvet 29c, 1700
Another small location, not far from the main station, with an outside seating area to contrast with the darker, more intimate interior.

Mikkeller Bar, Victoriagade 8b/c, 1650
Small, and thus often crowded, bar in fresh, modern style, opened close to the main station by Denmark's most celebrated brewer.

Taphouse, Lavendelstræde 15, 1462
Central bar, near the city hall, with no fewer than 61 taps. Tutored tastings are available.

Warpigs, Flæsketorvet 25–37, 1711
A joint venture between Mikkeller and US brewery Three Floyds, this large, often noisy brew pub in the Meatpacking district features long wooden tables, Texas barbecue food and 20 taps.

Brew It Yourself

In 2013, a Texas man came up with his own definition of the term local brewery when he found his own stomach was creating beer. Feeling somewhat disorientated, the 61-year-old man headed for the hospital where high quantities of *Saccharomyces cerevisiae* – brewer's yeast to you and me – were discovered in his digestive system. Working through the carbohydrates the man had consumed, the yeast had created enough alcohol to put him five times over the local driving limit. Effectively, he was suffering from a rare ailment known as 'auto brewery syndrome'. This explained why his wife constantly discovered him drunk at home, even though he swore to never having touched a drop. Fortunately, an anti-fungal treatment and a low-carbohydrate diet soon resolved the problem.

The Rise of Lager

The figures below show the percentage split of annual UK beer production between ale and lager over recent decades. They reveal how rapidly lager took over the market, although its share of sales has now flattened out.

	Ale*	Lager
1970	93.0	7.0
1980	69.3	30.7
1990	48.8	51.2
2000	36.8	63.2
2010	26.1	73.8
2014	25.2	74.8

* Includes stout. Source: *British Beer & Pub Association Statistical Handbook 2015*.

The Tax on Our Beer

Who pays the most beer tax? Comparative excise duty rates in Europe.

Country	Duty*	Country	Duty*
Finland	64.6	Austria	9.7
UK	52.2	Poland	9.0
Ireland	45.5	Belgium	8.9
Sweden	41.4	Malta	8.4
Slovenia	24.4	Portugal	7.8
Netherlands	15.3	Slovakia	7.2
Denmark	15.1	Latvia	6.3
France	14.9	Lithuania	6.3
Italy	14.7	Czech Republic	5.7
Estonia	14.6	Romania	4.3
Greece	12.6	Spain	4.0
Cyprus	12.1	Germany	3.8
Croatia	10.7	Luxembourg	3.8
Hungary	10.5	Bulgaria	3.7

* Pence per pint at 5% ABV.

Source: *British Beer & Pub Association Statistical Handbook 2015*.

The Strange Bottle Cap Heist

Shopkeepers in the German town of Mülheim were baffled in 2015 after a burglary at their premises. The burglars didn't attempt to steal money or goods from the store but simply made off with caps from more than 1,200 beer bottles – all of the same brand, König Pils. Not even the beer inside was touched. It was eventually deduced that the thieves must have been looking for caps printed with tokens that guaranteed prizes such as speakers and cordless drills in a brewery competition, leaving the brewery awaiting an unusually high number of applications from some claimants.

Restaurant Chain Beers

Arguably the best beer regularly available in major UK restaurant chains.

Restaurant	Beer
ASK Italian	Peroni Gran Riserva
Bella Italia	Menabrea
Bill's	Harviestoun Schiehallion
Brasserie Blanc	Sierra Nevada Pale Ale
Byron's	Thornbridge Jaipur*
Café Rouge	St Germain Page 24 Blonde
Carluccio's	Birra del Borgo ReAle
Chiquito	Fuller's London Pride
Chimichanga	Modelo Especial
Coast to Coast	Goose Island Honker's Ale
Côte Brasserie	Pelforth Blonde
Ed's Easy Diner	Samuel Adams Boston Lager
Frankie & Benny's	Samuel Adams Boston Lager
Garfunkel's	Meantime Pale Ale
Giggling Squid	Singha
Giraffe	Brooklyn Lager
Gourmet Burger Kitchen	BrewDog Punk IPA
Handmade Burger Co	Flying Dog Snake Dog IPA
Harry Ramsden's	Westerham Viceroy IPA
Jamie's Italian	Freedom Libertà†
La Tasca	Alhambra 1925 Reserva
La Viña	Alhambra 1925 Reserva

Las Iguanas	Estrella Inedit
Loch Fyne	Fyne Ales Highlander
Loungers	Bristol Beer Factory Cruiser Atlantic Pale Ale†
Maxwell's	Brooklyn Lager
Miller & Carter	Innis & Gunn Original
Nando's	Superbock
Piccolino	Peroni Gran Riserva
Pizza Express	Fuller's Honey Dew
Pizza Hut	San Miguel
Prezzo	Peroni Gran Riserva
Strada	Peroni Gran Riserva
TGI Fridays	Sierra Nevada Pale Ale
Thai Square	Singha
Turtle Bay	Guinness West Indies Porter
Veeno	Baladin Isaac
Wagamama	Hitachino Nest White Ale
Wahaca	Negra Modelo
YO! Sushi	Kagua Blanc
Zizzi	I Due Mastri Guru

Note: Some restaurants vary the drinks offering by location. Some also offer guest beers.

* Range also includes Beavertown Gamma Ray, BrewDog Dead Pony Club, Brooklyn Lager, Camden Hells Lager and Sierra Nevada Hop Hunter, plus beers from smaller breweries in some outlets. † House beer

---

It's the Law

Despite recent relaxation, the US state of Utah has some of the strangest rules regarding the service of alcohol, and beer in particular. For a start, no draught beer is allowed to be stronger than 4% ABV. Stronger bottled beers can be served but, if you're drinking in a restaurant that has started up since 2009, these must be opened behind a barrier, out of sight of the customer. Utah law also prohibits anyone from bringing alcohol into the state – unless they've just got off an international flight or are jointly resident in another state and have a permit. No free samples are allowed – meaning no sampler trays and promotions by breweries – and forget about ordering yourself more than a couple of beers as the law says only two alcoholic drinks can be put in front of a customer at any one time.

Beer Drinkers of the Year

The 'Beer Drinker of the Year' award is presented every summer by the All-Party Parliamentary Beer Group to the person who, in the opinion of the judges, has made a signal contribution to British life, with special reference to beer, during the previous year. Here are the winners to date.

1994 Rt. Hon. Kenneth Clarke QC MP (Chancellor of the Exchequer)
1995 Jack Charlton OBE (football manager)
1996 Anna Chancellor (actress)
1997 John Lowe OBE (darts player)
1998 John Cryne (retiring Chairman of CAMRA)
1999 Michael Parkinson OBE (journalist and talk show host)
2000 Edward Kelsey (aka 'Joe Grundy' of Radio 4's *The Archers*)
2001 Darren Gough (cricketer)
2002 HRH The Prince of Wales
2003 Nigel Jones MP (retiring Chairman of the All-Party Parliamentary Beer Group)
2004 Roger Protz (Editor, *Good Beer Guide*, and beer writer)
2005 Rt. Hon. Gordon Brown MP (Chancellor of the Exchequer)
2006 Andrew Flintoff (cricketer)
2007 Michel Roux (chef)
2008 Nick Hewer (PR consultant/TV personality)
2009 David and Robert Aynesworth (publicans)
2010 John Grogan (past Chairman of the All-Party Parliamentary Beer Group)
2011 Sriram Aylur (chef)
2012 Peter Hendy (London Transport commissioner)
2013 Rt. Hon. George Osborne MP (Chancellor of the Exchequer)
2014 Robert Humphreys (former Honorary Secretary of the All-Party Parliamentary Beer Group)
2015 *The Sun* newspaper
2016 Cathy Price (author of *The Red Lioness*)

CAMRA's National Beer Scoring System

To help CAMRA branches select pubs for the annual *Good Beer Guide*, beer drinkers can submit simple surveys of the beers they have sampled, rating them on a scale from 0 to 5. Information on how to do this can be found online at camra.org.uk/nbss. Here are the possible scores surveyors can give, together with a brief description of what each score actually implies.

0........................**No cask ale available.**
1........................**Poor** Beer that is anything from barely drinkable to drinkable with considerable resentment.
2........................**Average** Competently kept, drinkable pint but doesn't inspire in any way; not worth moving to another pub but you drink the beer without really noticing.
3........................**Good** Good beer in good form. You may cancel plans to move to the next pub. You want to stay for another pint and may seek out the beer again.
4........................**Very Good** Excellent beer in excellent condition.
5........................**Perfect** Probably the best you are ever likely to find. A seasoned drinker will award this score very rarely.

The US Beer Market

Remarkably for a country whose brewing industry was almost wiped out in the early 20th century by Prohibition, there are now more breweries in the USA than at any time in its history, as the following statistics reveal.

Microbreweries	2,397
Brewpubs	1,650
Regional craft breweries	178
Non-craft	44
Total	**4,269**

Figures given are for 2015. Source: Brewers Association.

UK Excise Duty Rates Since 1950

Excise duty is the tax paid by brewers on the beers they produce, a charge which is then passed on to customers as part of the price of a pint. The following figures show, in pence, the UK excise duty that has been levied over the years per pint, based on a beer with an original gravity of 1037.*

1950	3.29	1980	8.60
1959	2.58	1981	11.86
1961	2.84	1982	13.44
1964	3.23	1983	14.23
1965	3.62	1984	15.81
1966	3.99	1985	17.00
1968	4.39	1988	17.79
1973	2.91	1990	19.17
1974	3.77	1991	20.95
1975	5.51	1992	21.90
1976	6.38	1993	22.99
1977	7.01		

Excise duty, in pence, levied per pint for a beer of 4.0% ABV.[†]

1993	23.75	2008 (March)	34.00
1995	24.59	2008 (December)	36.71
1998	25.32	2009	37.44
1999	26.14	2010	39.37
2000	27.03	2011	42.21
2003	27.78	2012	44.35
2004	28.61	2013	43.44
2005	29.37	2014	42.58
2006	30.14	2015	41.74
2007	31.16		

Years shown are those when changes in duty rate took place. * Until 31 May 1993, duty on beer was levied according to the original gravity of the wort prior to pitching the yeast for fermentation. A wastage allowance of 6% was given, as not all the wort would have gone on to be finished beer. [†] Since 1 June 1993, excise duty has been based on the alcoholic strength of the finished beer.

In 2002, Progressive Beer Duty was introduced for brewers producing fewer than 30,000 hectolitres a year. In 2004, this threshold was extended to 60,000 hectolitres.

A Pint of Perry

On her Prismatic World Tour in 2014, singer Katy Perry took to swigging a glass of a beer as part of her stage act. After a few sips, she then passed the pint to a guy in the audience. Here are the beers she sampled on the UK section of the tour (attempting to find a beer that was popular locally).

Belfast .... Tennent's Lager
Birmingham .... Banks's Mild
Glasgow .... Tennent's Lager
Liverpool .... Liverpool Organic Brewery beer
London .... Fuller's London Pride
Manchester .... Holt's Two Hoots
Newcastle .... Newcastle Brown Ale
Nottingham .... Greene King Hardys & Hansons William Clark
Sheffield .... Bradfield Brewery beer

The Importance of Glassware

To understand how important glassware is to beer appreciation, take one beer and pour equal quantities into a straight half-pint glass and a good wine glass that tapers in towards the top. Without swirling the beers in the glasses (which would even things up), compare the aromas. It is remarkable how much more aroma the wine glass delivers. You can also try drinking the same beer out of a chunky half-pint mug and a delicate wine glass to see how the glass itself can be a barrier to flavour. With a thick glass, your mouth shapes differently when drinking, directing beer further back on the tongue, blocking some immediate work by your tastebuds and giving a duller taste sensation. Also, although glass has a neutral taste, that big chunk of material is intrusive, deflecting attention from the beer. The finer wine glass places the beer right at the front of the mouth, allowing all taste receptors to get in on the act.

From *So You Want to Be a Beer Expert?* (CAMRA Books) by Jeff Evans.

Self-Important Beers

There are some beers that appear to have a high opinion of themselves.

Beer	Brewery
Amazing Ale	Beeches
Brilliant Ale	Shepherd Neame
Dark & Delicious	Corvedale/Snowdonia
Dark & Handsome	Box Steam
Extra Special Bitter (ESB)	Fuller's
Genuine Stunning Strong Ale	Stringers
Maggs Magnificent Mild	West Berkshire
Marvellous Maple Mild	Brentwood
Stellar IPA	Ramsbottom
Sublime Stout	Fyne Ales
Superior London Porter	Brodie's
Wonderful	Wood's

The Most Popular American Hops

The major hop varieties grown today in the USA, by the area cultivated.

Variety	Hectares	Variety	Hectares
Cascade	2,849	Nugget	567
Centennial	2,105	Willamette	550
CTZ*	2,012	Apollo	405
Chinook	804	Bravo	297
Summit	656	Super Galena	212

Other hops 9,308

* Columbus, Tomahawk and Zeus, three closely related varieties that are grouped together for statistical purposes.

Figures relate to 2015. Source: Hopsteiner/International Hop Growers' Convention.

A Dozen Great British Beer Shops

1 **Beer Revolution**, The Old Storeroom, Hay Castle, Hay-on-Wye
   HR3 5DG. Tel. 07870 628097 beerrevolution.co.uk

2 **Favourite Beers**, 105 Hewlett Road, Cheltenham, Gloucestershire
   GL52 6BB. Tel. 01242 220485 favouritebeers.com

3 **Hop Hideout**, 448 Abbeydale Road, Sheffield S7 1FR.
   hophideout.co.uk

4 **Inn at Home**, 151 Bartholomew Street, Newbury, Berkshire
   RG14 5HB. innathome.co.uk

5 **Real Ale**, 371 Richmond Road, Twickenham TW1 2EF.
   Tel. 020 8892 3710 realale.com

6 **Southwick Brewhouse**, Southwick, Fareham, Hampshire PO17 6EB.
   Tel. 023 92 201133 southwickbrewhouse.co.uk

7 **Stirchley Wines & Spirits**, 1535–37 Pershore Road, Stirchley,
   Birmingham B30 2JH. Tel. 0121 459 9936
   stirchleywines.co.uk

8 **Tomlinsons Beer Shop**, 79 Castle Street, Inverness IV2 3EA.
   Tel. 01463 719858 tomlinsonsbeershop.co.uk

9 **Trembling Madness**, 48 Stonegate, York YO1 8AS.
   Tel. 01904 289848 tremblingmadness.co.uk

10 **Tucker's Maltings**, Teign Road, Newton Abbot, Devon TQ12 4AA.
   Tel. 01626 334734 tuckersmaltings.com

11 **We Brought Beer**, 78 St John's Hill, Clapham Junction, London
   SW11 1SF. Tel. 020 7228 4775
   webroughtbeer.co.uk/clapham-junction-shop/

12 **Westholme Store**, 26 Wallingford Road, Goring-on-Thames,
   Oxfordshire RG8 0BG. Tel. 01491 872619 beersnale.co.uk

American Beer Weeks

Month	City/State
January	Alaska
	San Francisco, California
	South Florida
February	Arizona
	New York City, New York
	Omaha, Nebraska
	Sacramento, California
March	Charlotte, North Carolina
	Colorado
	Tampa Bay, Florida
April	Madison, Wisconsin
	Milwaukee, Wisconsin
	Pittsburgh, Pennsylvania
	San Antonio, Texas
May	American Craft Beer Week (national)
	Albuquerque, New Mexico
	Asheville, North Carolina
	Chicago, Illinois
	Eugene, Oregon
	Minnesota
	Nevada
	Seattle, Washington
June	Alabama
	Cincinnati, Ohio
	Los Angeles, California
	Philadelphia, Pennsylvania
	Portland, Oregon
July	Ohio
August	St Louis, Missouri
September	Buffalo, New York
	Washington, DC
October	Baltimore, Maryland
	Cleveland, Ohio
November	Connecticut
	Massachusetts
	San Diego, California

The World's Top Beer-Drinking Nations

	Country	Litres per head		Country	Litres per head
1	Czech Republic	144.0	21	UK	66.2
2	Germany	107.0	22	Brazil	65.9
3	Austria	105.0	23	Canada	64.3
4	Poland	96.0	24	New Zealand	64.2
5	Lithuania	93.0	25	Denmark	63.0
6	Australia	84.0	26	Russia	62.1
7	Luxembourg	83.0	27	Hungary	60.0
8	Romania	81.0	28	South Africa	58.9
9	Finland	80.0	29	Ukraine	56.8
10	Ireland	79.0	30	Colombia	49.6
11	Latvia	78.0	31	Mexico	49.0
12	Slovenia	77.9	32	Argentina	43.1
13	Croatia	76.0	33	Japan	43.1
14	USA	76.0	34	South Korea	41.0
15	Spain	75.5	35	China	37.1
16	Bulgaria	74.0	36	Vietnam	33.5
17	Venezuela	73.8	37	Thailand	30.8
18	Belgium	72.0	38	France	29.6
19	Slovakia	72.0	39	Italy	29.2
20	Netherlands	69.9	40	Nigeria	15.2

Figures show annual beer consumption in 2013.

Source: *British Beer & Pub Association Statistical Handbook 2015*.

The End Product

Just when you thought novelty beers couldn't get any more weird up pop the Japanese and the Icelanders with two enticing options. The Sankt Gallen brewery in Japan's offering is called Un, Kono Kuro – basically meaning 'shit black'. That's not a flippant, self-effacing description of the beer: it sums up how the beer is made, for the brew contains coffee beans that have passed through the digestive system of an elephant and then been reclaimed from its deposits. Meanwhile, Brog brewery in Reykjavik has found an alternative use for animal droppings. Its Fenrir Nr. 26 beer features malt that has been lovingly dried over fires of sheep excrement.

The A–Z of Brewing

Kent-based artist Hugh Ribbans (hughribbans.com), who specialises in linocut work, has produced this wonderful illustration of various aspects of the beer-making process. The key to each of the letters is shown below.

Ale: a top-fermenting beer
Barley: the cereal most beer is made from
Cellar: the cool place where beer is stored
Dray: the traditional delivery vehicle for beer
Enjoy: the pleasure of a pint
Fermentation: the conversion of sugar to alcohol and carbon dioxide by yeast
Grist: the mix of grains used in a beer
Hops: the resinous plant that adds bitterness and other flavours to beer
Infusion: the process of mashing the grains to extract the starches
Jug: one way beer used to be served
Keg: a pressurised container for storing beer
Liquor: what brewers call water used for brewing
Malt: barley that has been prepared for brewing so that its starches can be extracted
Nidget: a type of hoe used to clear ground between rows of hops
Oast: a place where hops were traditionally dried
Publican: the person we rely on to look after and serve us beer
Quart: two pints please!
Racking: the process of filling casks or kegs
Stringing: setting up the strings that hops can grow around
Tankard: the traditional cup of cheer
Underback: a wort-holding vessel used between the mash tun and the copper
Venting: releasing excess carbonation from a cask
Well: the source of a brewery's water supply
XXX: an old form of indicating the strength of a beer
Yeast: the single-celled fungus responsible for fermentation
Zentner: a measurement of hop quantity, equivalent to 50 kilos

The Five Ages of Porter

The history of porter is long and complicated with the character of the drink changing as the basic ingredients and the way in which the beer was aged and blended before going on sale were altered over time. Beer historian Martyn Cornell in his book *Amber, Gold & Black* (The History Press, 2010) explains the development of this beer style in considerable detail, neatly summarising the evolution of porter in the following way.

'Palaeoporter' (c.1720–c.1740)
Brewed entirely from highly-dried brown malt; matured for a relatively short time in butts; strong and cloudy and quite likely with at least some smoky tang when young. Colour: dark brown

'Early mesoporter' (c.1740–c.1790)
Brewed entirely from brown malt; matured for a long time (up to two years) in vats; fine, clear and strong; some may have been sent out as new, or mild porter for mixing in the pot with stale, or matured porter. Colour: dark brown

'Late mesoporter' (c.1790–c.1820)
Generally brewed from a mixture of pale and brown malts, or pale, amber and brown malts; most sent out mild, the remainder vatted for up to two years before sending out to publicans as 'stale' or 'entire' for mixing with the old porter. Colour: variable but dark brown

'London neoporter' (c.1820 onwards)
Brewed from a mixture of pale malt, brown malt and black malt; still sent out as mild and stale, and mixed to the customer's taste by the publican. Colour: brown to black

'Irish neoporter' (c.1824 onwards)
Brewed from a mixture of pale malt and black malt. Sent out as 'low' (mature and nearly flat) or 'high' (freshly refermented and lively). Colour: black

CAMRA's Champion Winter Beers of Britain

Beers in the categories of Strong Milds/Old Ales, Stouts/Porters and Barley Wines/Strong Old Ales have been judged separately from the Champion Beer of Britain contest since 1996/7, with the overall winner declared Champion Winter Beer of Britain. Here are the winter champions to date.

1996/7	Hambleton Nightmare
1997/8	Nethergate Old Growler
1999	Dent T'Owd Tup
2000	Robinsons Old Tom
2001	Orkney Skull Splitter
2002	Wye Valley Dorothy Goodbody's Wholesome Stout
2003	Nethergate Old Growler
2004	Moor Old Freddy Walker
2005	Robinsons Old Tom
2006	Hogs Back A over T
2007	Green Jack Ripper
2008	Wickwar Station Porter
2009	Oakham Attila
2010	Elland 1872 Porter
2011	Hop Back Entire Stout
2012	Driftwood Alfie's Revenge
2013	Elland 1872 Porter
2014	Dunham Massey Dunham Porter
2015	Elland 1872 Porter
2016	Marble Chocolate Marble

The Number of Pubs in the UK

	England & Wales	Scotland	Northern Ireland	Total
1980	67,091	7,431	2,069	76,591
2000	77,876	7,571	1,802	87,249
2014	78,500	11,307*	1,475	91,282

Figures relate to public houses and hotels with full on-licences but do not include restaurants, clubs or off-licences. * Includes restaurants and hotels with restricted licences.
Source: *British Beer & Pub Association Statistical Handbook 2015.*

The Big Breakfast (and Dinner)

The JD Wetherspoon pub group runs more than 900 pubs across the UK, serving food and drink from morning (350,000 cooked breakfasts per week, including 35,000 eggs Benedict) to night (the group claims to be 'the nation's biggest curry house'). If you've ever wondered how much produce the company serves up every year, here comes your answer.

46 million free-range eggs
50 million Lincolnshire sausages
20 million burgers
6 million curries
50 million hot drinks

Five Highly Influential Beer Books

The Beer Drinker's Companion, by Frank Baillie (David & Charles, 1973)
When the *Good Beer Guide* first appeared in 1974, it included only an elementary listing of British breweries. A more comprehensive study, it advised, could be found in Frank Baillie's *Beer Drinker's Companion*. Baillie, it was said, had drunk every draught beer available, so there was instant authority in his writing. All Britain's independent breweries of the time were described in detail, with basic tasting notes.

The Death of the English Pub, by Christopher Hutt (Arrow, 1973)
Just what are the big brewers planning for YOUR local? Is your pint as strong as it used to be? How polluted is your pint? These were just three of the questions posed by this early insight into the manipulative ways of the British brewing industry. Chris Hutt – later a national chairman of CAMRA – lifted the lid on how the traditional pub experience was being eroded in the name of quick profit in the early 1970s.

Beer and Skittles, by Richard Boston (Collins, 1976)
An early celebration of the joys of pub life by a *Guardian* beer columnist. While romping through the history and traditions, Richard Boston also castigated those who were seeking to destroy all that was good about this wonderful British institution. Among reflections on pub games, clientele and the liquid in the glass, Boston also offered cooking-with-beer recipes.

The World Guide to Beer, by Michael Jackson (Mitchell Beazley, 1977)
While CAMRA was doing battle with the brewing industry in the UK, journalist Michael Jackson turned his attention to the bigger picture and put together the first comprehensive, full-colour survey of beer around the world. In the days when travel was expensive and borders not so easy to cross, Jackson somehow found a way to introduce readers to the delights of Belgian lambics, true Czech pilsners and even American beer before the dawn of the craft beer movement. Indeed, it was this very book that – many acknowledge – provided the encouragement and blueprint for home brewers in the US to raise their game and turn professional.

Pulling a Fast One, by Roger Protz (Pluto, 1978)
In *Pulling a Fast One*, veteran campaigner Roger Protz fired his first salvo against the brewing industry. Like Chris Hutt's contribution, this book ruthlessly exposed the devious practices of the big brewers In the 1970s. The subtitle – 'What Brewers Have Done to Your Beer' – says it all, summarising how Protz dissected the rationalisation, short-termism and cynicism that was still threatening the British beer and pub experience several years after the foundation of CAMRA.

See Further Reading (pages 144–5) for other important beer books to consult.

The Continual Demise of the Pub

The shocking number of pubs that are closing every single week in the UK.

Period	Closures*
September 2011–March 2012	12
March 2012–September 2012	18
September 2012–March 2013	26
March 2013–December 2013	28
December 2013–June 2014	31
June 2014–December 2014	29
December 2014–June 2015	29
June 2015–December 2015	27
December 2015–June 2016	21

* Net weekly closures. Source: The Campaign for Real Ale.

British Beer Imports

	Country	Thousand hl
1	Ireland	2,546.5
2	Italy	1,589.0
3	Netherlands	1,066.4
4	France	861.5
5	Germany	492.4
6	Mexico	408.6
7	Belgium & Luxembourg	263.4
8	Czech Republic	217.7
9	USA	79.7
10	Sweden	73.0
11	Spain	72.8
12	Poland	68.2
13	Cyprus	67.9
14	Portugal	28.3
15	Canada	25.1
	Other countries	672.4

Figures given are for 2014. Source: *British Beer & Pub Association Statistical Handbook 2015.*

Brewing: the Soul of a Pub Estate

'History shows that once companies close their breweries they lose their souls and a culture which we believe adds value to the way pubs are run', so claimed Fergus McMullen, production director of McMullen's, in May 2006 at the opening of a new £1 million brewery at its Hertford site. Although the brewery was smaller than the original brewhouse, it allowed the company to stay in brewing rather than just become a pub company. The same month it was announced that Young's brewery in Wandsworth was to close, with production of its beers transferred to Bedford in a joint venture with Charles Wells called Wells & Young's. The joint venture no longer exists. Charles Wells retains the brewery; Young's now only runs pubs.

The Astonishing Rise of British Brewing

Do the math! The number of operational breweries listed in the *Good Beer Guide* over a selection of years, since the publication of the first edition.

Edition	Independents	National/Internationals	Total
1 (1974)	91	50	141
10 (1983)	191	47	238
20 (1993)	224	43	267
30 (2003)	431	16	447
40 (2013)	1002*	7	1009
44 (2017)	1538	n/a	1538

* Includes a small number of breweries sharing facilities.

Figures include brew pubs. Split of Nationals/Internationals not provided after 2013.

The Great Wisconsin Hop Crash

Making an instant fortune from your land is a concept normally associated with the discovery of oil or gold but, in 19th-century America, it was hops that provided unexpected prosperity. When aphids wiped out much of the hop crop in New York state during the 1860s, farmers in Sauk County, Wisconsin, sensed an opportunity. Hops being hard to come by, their price soared, rising from around 20 cents per pound to top, at one point, 70 cents per pound. People rushed to plant the crop, abandoning less profitable staples such as vegetables and dairy products that now had to be brought into the region. Some raised money to buy farms that then proceeded to pay for themselves with just one crop, but it couldn't last. In 1868, with so many producers turning over their land to hops, and New York farmers back in business, there were too many hops on the market and the price crashed to around 5 cents per pound or less. Many people who had made fortunes lost them just as quickly. Posh houses and fancy carriages were swiftly repossessed as nervous banks called in loans and hop growing in the region was returned to a more sustainable level.

Television's Fictional Beers and Breweries

Beer/Brewery	Programme
Alamo Beer	King of the Hill
Ashbury Export	Shameless
Bendërbräu	Futurama
Black Death Malt Liquor	WKRP in Cincinnati
Black Frost Beer	Buffy the Vampire Slayer
Canoga Beer	Roseanne
Causton Ales	Midsomer Murders
Chapston's	Where the Heart Is
Churchill's	EastEnders
Coops	Magnum, PI
Dharma Initiative Beer	Lost
Duff Beer	The Simpsons
Ephraim Monk	Emmerdale
Flagler Beer	Magnum, PI
Fudd Beer	The Simpsons
Hammerstein Beer	Two and a Half Men
Heisler Beer*	Various US series
Jekyll Island Lager*	Various US series
Leopard Lager	Red Dwarf
Luxford & Copley	EastEnders
Monkeyshine Beer	Friends
Newton & Ridley	Coronation Street
Olde Fortran	Futurama
Pawtucket Patriot Ale	Family Guy
Penzburg*	Various US series
Red Tick Beer	The Simpsons
Romulan Ale	Star Trek
Shotz	Laverne & Shirley
Stelberg Louis	Shameless

* Beers created as set props.

British Brewery Name Changes

The following breweries have all changed their names at some point, either through mergers or takeovers or simply as a rebranding exercise.

Old Name	New Name	Old Name	New Name
Alcazar	Basin City	Jersey	Liberation
Alehouse	Verulam	Kite	Glamorgan
Anglo Dutch	Partners	Leek	Staffordshire
Ann Street	Liberation	Lidstone's	Wensleydale
Artisan	Pipes	Longden	Shropshire Brewer
Banks & Taylor	B&T		
Barron's	Exe Valley	McLaughlin's	Camden Town
Big End	Daleside	Matthews	Dawkins
Bramcote	Castle Rock	Mitchell Krause	Tractor Shed
Bridgewater	Blueball	Mulligans	One Mile End
Brew Company	Exit 33	O'Hanlons	Hanlons
Brew Star	Anarchy	Oak	Phoenix
Brewmeister	Keith	Paradise	North Wales
Brothers	Freedom	Pennine	Rossendale
Bunces	Stonehenge	Preseli	Tenby
Conquest	Whitby	Princetown	Dartmoor
Dickensian	Target	Quay	Dorset
East Stratton	Black Bear	Royal Clarence	RCH
Eastwood & Sanders	Elland	Shoulder of Mutton	Weldon
		Sky's Edge	Exit 33
Farmer's Ales	Maldon	Spencer's	G2
Flagship	Nelson	Spinning Dog	Hereford
Four Rivers	Hadrian Border	Sutton	South Hams
Fowler's	Prestonpans	Topsham & Exminster	Exeter
Frys	Bude		
Gargoyles	Isca	Town Mill	Lyme Regis
Gidley's	Black Tor	Traditional Scottish Ales	Black Wolf
Glenny	Wychwood		
Growler	Nethergate	Vale of Glamorgan	VOG
Gundog	Acton	Wapping	Baltic Fleet
Highland	Swannay	Woodfarm	Kendrick's
Highwood	Tom Wood	William Worthington's	Heritage
Hillside	Deeside		

CAMRA's Pub Design Awards

With English Heritage, CAMRA recognises good pub architecture through Pub Design Awards, which are presented in the following five categories.

Year	Best New Build Pub	Best Refurbishment
1986	Barn Owl, Northampton	Minerva, Hull/Chandos, London WC2
1987	–	–
1988	No awards	
1989	–	Sun Inn, Barnes/Bow Bar, Edinburgh
1990	–	White Hart, Littleton-on-Severn
1991	Smiles Brewery Tap, Bristol	–
1992	Blind Jack's, Knaresborough	Anchor, Oxford
1993	–	IW Frazier's Cumberland Bar, Edinburgh
1994	–	Cain's Brewery Tap, Liverpool
1995	–	Seahorse, Bristol
1996	–	–
1997	–	Bread & Roses, London SW4
1998	Wharf, Walsall	Stalybridge Station Buffet
1999	–	Dispensary, Liverpool
2000	–	–
2001	–	Burton Bridge Brewery Tap, Burton upon Trent
2002	Manor Barn Farm, Southfleet	Test Match, West Bridgford
2003	–	Wortley Almshouses, Peterborough
2004	No awards	
2005	Zerodegrees, Bristol	Racecourse, Salford
2006	–	Prince of Wales, Herne Bay
2007	Black Horse Inn, Walcote	Weaver Hotel, Runcorn
2008	Zerodegrees, Reading	Princess Louise, London/Castle Inn, Bradford on Avon
2009	–	Sutton Hall, Macclesfield
2010	–	Bell Inn, Rode
2011	No awards	
2012	–	Joule's Brewery Tap, Market Drayton
2013	Hall & Woodhouse, Portishead	White Swan, Shawell
2014	No awards	
2015	–	Castle, Edgehill/Old Bridge Inn, Kirkstall
2016	Admiral Collingwood, Ilfracombe	Dun Cow, Sunderland

* Sponsored by English Heritage and rewards conservation of a pub's best architectural features and preservation of its fabric.

** Award named after a former CAMRA chairman and presented for the best street-corner local, if worthy. Note: Awards are not made in every category every year.

Best Conversion to Pub	Conservation Award*	Joe Goodwin Award**
–	–	Crown Posada, Newcastle upon Tyne/Scotch Piper, Lydiate
–	–	Golden Cross, Cardiff
–	–	Junction, Southampton
–	–	Queen's Head, Stockport
–	Mill of the Black Monks, Monks Bretton	–
–	–	–
Truscott, London EC2	Fox & Anchor, London EC1	–
–	Bridge Inn, Rochdale	Bridge Inn, Rochdale
Rothwells, Manchester/ Courtyard, Leeds	Counting House, Pontefract	–
Commercial Rooms, Bristol	Commercial Rooms, Bristol	Vine, Brierly Hill
Frazer's Bar, Edinburgh	–	–
–	Olde Trip to Jerusalem, Nottingham	–
Billiard Hall, West Bromwich/ Half Moon, London E1	–	Dispensary, Liverpool
Sedge Lynn, Manchester	Phoenix, York	Monkey, Crewe
Porterhouse, London	Bull & Butcher, Turville	Merchants Arms, Bristol
Gatekeeper, Cardiff	Bath Hotel, Sheffield	Holt's Railway, Didsbury
Smiths of Bourne, Lincolnshire	Bell Inn, Nottingham	–
Yorkshire Terrier, York	Prestoungrange Gothenberg, Prestonpans	Yarborough Hunt, Brigg
Works, Sowerby Bridge	Three Pigeons, Halifax	Prince of Wales, Herne Bay/ Three Pigeons, Halifax
Tobie Norris, Stamford	Weaver Hotel, Runcorn	–
–	–	–
Brewery Tap, Chester	Brewery Tap, Chester	–
Sheffield Tap, Sheffield	Sportsman, Huddersfield	Queen's Head, Burnham on Crouch
Drop Forge, Birmingham	Magpie, Carlisle/Prince Rupert, Newark	–
York Tap, York	Albion Ale House, Conwy	Cat's Back, Putney/Albion Ale House, Conwy
–	Castle, Edgehill	–
Chief Justice of the Common Pleas, Keswick	Dun Cow, Sunderland	Bevy, Brighton

The Top Ten Individual American Brewpubs

	Brewery (State)	US Barrels*
1	Boundary Bay Brewery & Bistro (Oregon)	6,147
2	Great Northern Brewing Co (Montana)	6,000
3	Crux Fermentation Project (Oregon)	5,870
4	Right Brain Brewery (Michigan)	4,777
5	Warped Wing Brewing Co (Ohio)	4,700
6	Brewery Vivant (Michigan)	4,687
7	North Country Brewing Co (Pennsylvania)	4,680
8	Icicle Brewing Co (Washington)	4,654
9	Petoskey Brewing (Michigan)	4,625
10	Market Garden Brewery (Ohio)	4,500

* Annual sales. Figures given are for 2015. Source: Brewers Association.

International Beer Challenge

The International Beer Challenge is a major competition for packaged beer (bottle and can) that is staged in London each year and closely allied to the trade magazine *Off Licence News*. Gold, silver and bronze awards are made in various classes but a supreme champion beer is always selected, too. Below is a list of the supreme champions in recent years.

2003	Weihenstephaner Hefeweissbier
2004	Innis & Gunn Oak Aged Beer
2005	Rogue Mocha Porter
2006	O'Hanlon's Thomas Hardy's Ale
2007	Deschutes The Abyss
2008	St Austell Admiral's Ale
2009	Weihenstephaner Hefeweissbier
2010	Boston Beer Samuel Adams Utopias 2009
2011	Kernel Export Stout
2012	Harveys Prince of Denmark
2013	Redoak Special Reserve
2014	Redoak Chateau Sour
2015	Baden Baden Witbier
2016	Prancing Pony India Red Ale

Off Flavours

Ever wondered why beer doesn't always taste great? There are plenty of things that can go wrong during the brewing process and the subsequent storage and service of a beer but these are the most common off flavours that you may come across, together with a likely explanation of the cause.

Flavour	Common Cause*	Technical Term
Baby Vomit	Bacterial infection	Butyric Acid
Butterscotch	Fermentation defect	Diacetyl
Cardboard/Wet Paper	Oxygen contamination	Oxidation
Cheese	Stale hops/bacterial infection	Isovaleric Acid
Cooked Vegetables	Slow wort cooling	Dimethyl Sulphide (DMS)
Disinfectant	Chlorine contamination	Chlorophenol
Farmyard	Fermentation defect	4-Ethyl Phenol
Green apple	Fermentation defect	Acetaldehyde
Harsh Dryness	Over-sparging	Astringency
Heat	Fermentation defect	Alcohol
Marmite	Yeast breakdown	Autolysis
Metallic	Contact with iron	Metallic
Mouldy	Poorly-stored grains	Fungal contamination
Plastic	Chlorine contamination	Chlorophenol
Skunky	Exposure to light	Isopentyl Mercaptan
Solvent	Fermentation defect	Ethyl Acetate
Sourness	Bacterial infection	Acidity
Soy Sauce	Yeast breakdown	Autolysis
Sulphur	Fermentation defect	Hydrogen Sulphide
Sweat	Fermentation defect	Caprylic Acid
Sweetcorn/tomatoes	Slow wort cooling	Dimethyl Sulphide (DMS)
Vinegar	Bacterial infection	Acidity

* There is often more than one cause of the problem.

Note that not all these flavours are always unwanted. Some beer styles are deliberately sour, for example, and others can acceptably feature a little DMS or diacetyl.

Extracted from *So You Want to Be a Beer Expert?* (CAMRA Books) by Jeff Evans.

Beer: the Low Sugar Option

At a time when the sugar content of drinks is under scrutiny, it is worth considering that beer contains less sugar than many other products, alcoholic or not. Prior to fermentation, the wort for a beer naturally includes a lot of sugar but this sugar is primarily in the form of maltose, which is almost entirely eaten up by the yeast during the fermentation process. Consequently, beer typically contains less than 1g of sugar per 100 ml (1.5g for strong beers), a lower figure than found in wine or cider, and far, far lower than the sugar content of Coca-Cola (10.6g per 100 ml).

Sources: *A Healthy Perspective on Beer* (British Beer & Pub Association, 2016); Coca-Cola website.

American Breweries of the Year

The Great American Beer Festival, held every autumn in Denver, Colorado, incorporates a major beer competition, attracting thousands of entries from American breweries. Based on medals awarded to beers in the competition, awards are made to the most successful breweries, of varying sizes, from large to very small. Here are the most recent winners.

Year	Large	Mid-Size	Small	Very Small
2006	Pabst (IL)	New Glarus (WI)	Bear Republic (CA)	–
2007	Pabst (IL)	Firestone Walker (CA)	Port & Lost Abbey (CA)	
2008	Anheuser-Busch (MO)	Pyramid (WA)	AleSmith (CA)	
2009	Coors (CO)	Flying Dog (MD)	Dry Dock (CO)	
2010	Blue Moon (CO)	Utah (UT)	Mad River (CA)	–
2011	Pabst (CA)	Firestone Walker (CA)	Chuckanut (WA)	–
2012	Pabst (CA)	Tröegs (PA)	Funkwerks (CO)	–
2013	SandLot (CO)	Firestone Walker (CA)	Devils Backbone (VA)	Baker City (OR)
2014	AC Golden (CO)	Devils Backbone (VA)	Marble (NM)	Draught Works (MT)
2015	Pabst (CA)	Firestone Walker (CA)	Port City (VA)	Rip Current (CA)

State abbreviations above are as follows: IL Illinois, WI Wisconsin, CA California, MO Missouri, WA Washington, CO Colorado, MD Maryland, UT Utah, PA Pennsylvania, VA Virginia, OR Oregon, NM New Mexico, MT Montana.

Capital Beer: Brussels

Five beer venues you have to visit when staying in the capital of Europe.

Bier Circus, Rue de l'Enseignement 57, 1000
Excellent beer list plus inventive food in an attractive corner café.

Delirium Café, 4 Impasse de la Fidelité, 1000
Busy cellar bar noted for its gigantic selection of bottles (more than 2,000), just off the touristy Rue des Bouchers.

Dynamo Bar de Soifs, Chaussée d'Alsemberg 130, St Gilles, 1060
A recent arrival in the craft beer-bar idiom, south of the centre near Parc de Forest.

Moeder Lambic Fontainas, Place Fontainas 8, 1000
Modern-styled, city-centre sister of the well-established and renowned Moeder Lambic bar, conveniently close to the Grand Place.

Poechenellekelder, Rue du Chêne 5, 1000
Surprisingly untouristy bar alongside the Mannekin Pis, housing some of the little boy's clothes.

Wood You Believe It?

Beer from the wood is no longer a thing of the past. Metal casks may have taken over as the containers of choice for most breweries during the 20th century, but one pub is determined to turn back the clock and give drinkers a chance to discover how beer used to taste. The Junction at Castleford, Yorkshire, has its own supply of wooden casks specially made by master cooper Alastair Simms and it sends these to local breweries to be filled. The beers are then served alongside Old Brewery Bitter from Samuel Smith, which the brewery only ever delivers in wood, to present one of the UK's most unusual beer selections. The annual Woodfest held here at Easter takes the idea to a new level, with even more beers on offer.

Some Important Dates in the History of Hops

When popular hop varieties were bred or (R) released for commercial use.

1700s	Golding	1983	Crystal
1875	Fuggle		Liberty
1911	WGV (Whitbread Golding		Mount Hood
	Variety)	1984	Sorachi Ace
1919	Brewers Gold	1985	Chinook (R)
1927	Bramling Cross	1987	Pacific Gem (R)
1934	Northern Brewer	1990	Centennial
1951	Progress (R 1964)		Sterling (R 1998)
1953	Pride of Ringwood	1995	First Gold
1956	Cascade (R 1972)		Sovereign
1968	Galena (R 1978)	1996	Admiral (R)
1970	Northdown (R)		Phoenix
	Nugget (R 1983)	2000	Nelson Sauvin (R)
1972	Challenger (R)		Pilgrim (R)
	Green Bullet (R)		Simcoe (R)
	Target (R)	2001	Pilot (R)
1974	Centennial (R 1990)	2003	Summit (R)
1976	Willamette (R)	2004	Boadicea (R)
1978	Galena	2008	Citra (R)
	Perle (R)	2012	Mosaic (R)
1980	Magnum	2014	Olicana (R)

Sources: *The Hop Guide* (National Hop Association of England); charlesfaram.co.uk; nzhops.co.nz; Yakima Chief Inc. *Hop Varietal Guide 2013*.

Going on a Bender

In old money, a silver sixpence was commonly known as a 'bender', because the silver content of the coin made it easily twisted by hand. At some point in time, sixpence, rather conveniently, would also have been enough money for someone to have a pretty good time, buying enough beer in a tavern to ensure a happy state at the end of the evening. Thus, it is said by some, the phrase 'going on a bender' came into existence.

Who Drinks the Most Draught Beer?

The percentage of overall national beer sales taken up by draught beer.

Country	%	Country	%
Ireland	61	Bulgaria	14
UK	46	Italy	14
Czech Republic	42	Finland	12
Slovakia	33	Ukraine	12
Belgium	29	Hungary	10
Netherlands	26	Lithuania	10
Spain	26	Canada	10
Australia	22	USA	10
Japan	19	Slovenia	6
France	17	Poland	5
Denmark	16	Croatia	4
Germany	15	Romania	4
South Korea	15	China	2

Figures given are for 2013. Source: *British Beer & Pub Association Statistical Handbook 2015*.

Variety Is the Spice of Beer Life

One of the beauties of real beer is that it varies so much from brewery to brewery. Many people are narrow-minded enough to believe that only the beer they grew up with is any good – but the truth is that all real ales can be excellent when properly looked after by the landlord. If you are not prepared to accept variety, then this guide may be of little use to you.

From the introduction to the first edition of the *Good Beer Guide* (1974).

Thirty Years of Major UK Brewery Closures

The beer world is in a continual state of flux. Hundreds of exciting new breweries have arrived to brighten up the UK brewing scene in recent years but, unfortunately, we have also lost many substantial breweries over the last three decades. Here's a list of the biggest casualties of the changing face of British beer and the years in which they were closed.

1987 .... Dryborough, Edinburgh (Grand Metropolitan)
Rayments, Furneaux Pelham (Greene King)

1988 ....Chester's, Salford (Whitbread)
Paines, St Neots (Tolly Cobbold)
Theakston, Carlisle (Matthew Brown)
Theakston, Workington (Scottish & Newcastle)
Wem, Shropshire (Greenalls)
Wethered, Marlow (Whitbread)

1989 .... Davenports, Birmingham (Greenalls)
Truman, London (Grand Metropolitan)

1990 .... Crown, Pontyclun (Guinness)
Fremlins, Faversham (Whitbread)
Higsons, Liverpool (Whitbread – later re-opened as Cains)

1991 .... Matthew Brown, Blackburn (Scottish & Newcastle)
Greenalls, Warrington (ceased brewing)
Hansons, Dudley (Wolverhampton & Dudley)
Hartleys, Ulverston (Robinsons)
Preston Brook, Runcorn (Bass)
Romford (Allied Breweries)
Shipstone's, Nottingham (Greenalls)
Springfield, Wolverhampton (Bass)

1993 .... Exchange, Sheffield (Whitbread)

1994 .... Heriot, Edinburgh (Bass)
Hope, Sheffield (Bass)

1996 .... Home, Nottingham (Scottish & Newcastle)
Plympton, Plymouth (Carlsberg-Tetley)
Tetley Walker, Warrington (Carlsberg-Tetley)
Webster's, Halifax (Scottish & Newcastle)

1997 .... Gibbs Mew, Salisbury (ceased brewing)

1998 .... Cheltenham (Whitbread)
Crown Buckley, Llanelli (Brains)

Morrells, Oxford (ceased brewing)
Ruddles, Oakham (Morland)
1999 .... Alloa (Carlsberg-Tetley)
Brains, Cardiff (brewing moved to former Bass site)
Cannon, Sheffield (Bass)
Courage, Bristol (Scottish & Newcastle)
Maclay's, Alloa (ceased brewing)
Mitchell's, Lancaster (ceased brewing)
Vaux, Sunderland (ceased brewing)
Wards, Sheffield (Vaux)
2000 .... King & Barnes, Horsham (Hall & Woodhouse)
Morland, Abingdon (Greene King)
Ushers, Trowbridge (ceased brewing)
Wrexham Lager (Carlsberg-Tetley)
2001 .... Mansfield (Wolverhampton & Dudley)
2002 .... Brakspear, Henley-on-Thames (ceased brewing)
Cape Hill, Birmingham (Coors)
Castle Eden (brewing moved to Camerons in Hartlepool)
2003 .... Thomas Hardy, Dorchester (brewing moved to
Burtonwood)
Tolly Cobbold, Ipswich (brands sold to Ridley's)
2004 .... Fountain, Edinburgh (Scottish & Newcastle)
2005 .... Boddingtons, Manchester (InBev)
Park Royal, London (Guinness)
Redruth, Cornwall (ceased brewing)
Tyne, Newcastle upon Tyne (Scottish & Newcastle)
2006 .... Gale's, Horndean (Fuller's)
Hardys & Hansons, Nottingham (Greene King)
Ridley's, Hartford End (Greene King)
Young's, Wandsworth (brewing merged with Charles Wells)
2010 .... Dunston (Heineken UK)
Highgate, Walsall (ceased brewing)
Reading (Heineken UK)
2011 .... Tetley, Leeds (Carlsberg UK)
2013 .... Cains, Liverpool (ceased brewing)
2015 .... Alton (Molson Coors)
Stag, Mortlake (AB InBev)

Names in brackets indicate the company that closed the brewery.

Head Brewers of Major British Breweries

Adnams	Fergus Fitzgerald	Holden's	Roger Bennett
Arkell's	Alex Arkell	Holt's	Phil Parkinson
Banks's	Tom Spencer	Hook Norton	James Clarke
Batemans	Martin Cullimore	Hop Back	Steve Wright
Batham's	Martin Birch	Hydes	Paul Jefferies
Beavertown	Jenn Merrick	Jennings	Jeremy Pettman
Belhaven	Alan McLaren	Lees	Michael Lees-Jones
Black Sheep	Alan Dunn	McMullen	Chris Evans
Brains	Bill Dobson	Marston's	Patrick McGinty
BrewDog	Stewart Bowman	Meantime	Ciaran Giblin
Caledonian	Ian Kennedy	Palmers	Darren Batten
Camden Town	Rob Topham	Ringwood	Jeff Drew
Camerons	Martin Dutoy	Robinsons	Martyn Weeks
Coors (Burton)	Andrew Robinson	St Austell	Roger Ryman
Donnington	James Arkell	Sharp's	Andrew Madden
Elgood's	Alan Pateman	Shepherd Neame	Richard Frost
Everards	Graham Giblett	Timothy Taylor	Andrew Leman
Felinfoel	John Reed	Thornbridge	Rob Lovatt
Fuller's	John Keeling	Thwaites	Brian Yorston
Greene King	Craig Bennet	Wadworth	Colin Oke
Hall & Woodhouse	Toby Heasman	Charles Wells	Karl Ottomar
Harveys	Miles Jenner	Wychwood	Jeff Drew

Details correct as of June 2016.

A Pint and a Punt

Some British racecourses that now stage annual beer festivals on racedays.

Ascot	October
Newbury	April
Newcastle	June
Newmarket	September
Nottingham	May
Southwell	December
Uttoxeter	November

Spin-Off Breweries and Alternative Ranges

Some breweries offer beers under a different brand name, perhaps to trial experimental brews or to differentiate the range from their regular beers.

Brewery	Spin-Off/Alternative
Adnams	Jack Brand
Bath	Beerd
Black Sheep	My Generation
Clark's	Merrie City
George's	Hop Monster
Harveys	County Town
Marston's	Revisionist
Mordue	Panda Frog
Rooster's	Outlaw
Shepherd Neame	Whitstable Bay
Thwaites	Crafty Dan
Verulam	Ale Craft
West Berkshire	Renegade
Windsor & Eton	Uprising
XT	Animal

Some Alternative Uses for Hops

Food	Hop shoots have been likened in flavour to asparagus or samphire
Medicine	Hops, known for relaxant and soporific qualities, are made into pillows*
Skin Treatment	Hops act as an exfoliate, hence the use of beer in some spa treatments
Textiles	Hop stalks can be treated to create fibres

* Other health claims include the value of hops as an anti-inflamatory and anti-oxidant agent, as well as their potential cancer-fighting properties.

The UK's Most Successful Brewers and Beers

Based on results collated from CAMRA's annual Champion Beer of Britain and Champion Winter Beer of Britain contests, here is confirmation of the UK's most successful brewers and cask beers. The statistics shown are correct up to and including both Champion Beer competitions for 2016.

Most Supreme Champion Titles

Brewery	Wins	Last Win
Fuller's	5	1989*
Timothy Taylor	5	2014
Elland	4	2015†
Coniston	2	2012
Crouch Vale	2	2006
Nethergate	2	2003‡
Robinsons	2	2005‡
Thwaites	2	1980*
Woodforde's	2	1996

* Includes one shared title.

† Includes three Champion Winter Beer of Britain titles.

‡ Champion Winter Beer of Britain titles.

Most Category Wins

Brewery	Wins	Last Win
Timothy Taylor	14	2016
Fuller's	13	2007
Batemans	10	2005
Woodforde's	8	2005
Hop Back	6	2011
Oakham	6	2014
Cairngorm	5	2014
Elland	5	2016
Gale's	5	2006
Harveys	5	2015
Nethergate/Growler	5	2013
RCH	5	2010
Robinsons	5	2010
Theakston	5	2000

Dark Star	4	2015
Lees	4	2015
Purple Moose	4	2015
Adnams	3	2003
Ansells	3	1987
Cheriton	3	2003
Coach House	3	1994
Hogs Back	3	2013
Marble	3	2016
Mighty Oak	3	2011
Mordue	3	2013
O'Hanlon's	3	2007
Ridley's	3	1995
Salopian	3	2014
Surrey Hills	3	2016
Thwaites	3	1986
Titanic	3	2015
Triple fff	3	2008
Wye Valley	3	2008
Young's	3	1999

Most Successful Beers*

Beer	Wins	Last Win
Timothy Taylor Landlord	9	2010
Fuller's ESB	7	1991
Batemans XXXB	5	1997
Elland 1872 Porter	5	2016
Theakston Old Peculier	5	2000
Hop Back Summer Lightning	4	2001
Worthington's White Shield	4	2013
Cairngorm Trade Winds	3	2006
Gale's Festival Mild	3	2006
Marble Chocolate Marble	3	2016
Nethergate Old Growler	3	2003†
Woodforde's Headcracker	3	2003
Woodforde's Wherry	3	2005

* Based on category wins.

† Includes one shared title.

Themes Followed by Breweries for Beer Names

Brewery	Theme	Brewery	Theme
Atomic	nuclear terms	Musket	military history
Beartown	bears	Nelson	naval concepts
Biggar	Barrow shipbuilding	Old Chimneys	rare wildlife
Blackhill	Durham coal seams	Old Dairy	milk bottle caps
Blackjack	playing cards	Middle Earth	Tolkien
Blue Bell Brewhouse	motorcycles	Milton	myths, legends and gods
Borough	coal and steel	Moorhouse's	witchcraft
Bosun's	naval concepts	Out There	1950s space race
Box Steam	steam engines	Otley	the letter O
Bryncelyn	Buddy Holly	Paradigm	corporate jargon
Cheddar	local cave network	Rail Ale	railways
Cotleigh	birds of prey	Red Rock	coastal terms
Cryptic	puzzles	Roseland	local birds
Cwm Rhondda	coal mining	Scribbler's	classic novels
Dancing Duck	ducks	Shortts Farm	music
DarkTribe	naval concepts	Shropshire Brewer	local legends
Deeside	Scottish/Pictish kings	Silverstone	motor racing
Derventio	Ancient Rome	Spire	music
Deva Craft	Ancient Rome	Stamps	postage stamps
Dickens	Dickens characters	Storm	meteorological terms
Double Top	Darts	Target	Shropshire legends
Dowbridge	Roman Britain	Thames Side	Thames birds
Funfair	fairground rides	Three Bs	weaving terms
Fuzzy Duck	Spoonerisms	Titanic	RMS Titanic
Glastonbury	Arthurian legend	Triple fff	rock music tracks
Golden Duck	local cricket	Trinity	rugby league
Goffs	chivalry	Two Cocks	English Civil War
Gun	firearms and weaponry	Uley	pigs
Gun Dog	dogs	Ulverston	Laurel & Hardy
Hambleton	horses	Unsworth's Yard	local history
Hesket Newmarket	fells	Wantsum	Kent history
Jollyboat	naval concepts	Watermill	dogs
Kirkstall	Kirkstall Abbey	Wild Card	playing cards
Longhill	wind	Wolf	wild dogs
Mallard	ducks	Wooden Hand	pirates
Merry Miner	coal mining	Yetman's	colours

Early Warnings

The first edition of the *Good Beer Guide*, published in 1974, included a very rudimentary, two-page listing of the UK's breweries, with each brewery summed up succinctly in one line of text. Most of the descriptions centred on the quality of the ale and whether gas was added to force it to the bar. Not all these descriptions were complimentary, as the following shows. Thankfully, breweries that survive (or have been revived) from this list are now irreproachable when it comes to their cask ales and their dispense!

Everards, Burton-on-Trent: Not generally recommended.
Gibbs Mew, Salisbury: A disaster.
Holden, Woodsetton: Too much gassy beer.
Mitchells & Butlers, Birmingham: A bad bet.
Paine, St Neots: A complete waste of time.
Phipps, Northampton: Don't bother.
John Smith, Tadcaster: Deteriorating.
Truman, London: Steer well clear.
Watney, London and Norwich: Avoid at all costs.*
Welsh, Cardiff: A shadow of the beer it has replaced.

* The original wording was 'Avoid like the plague'. This was withdrawn on legal advice.

The Most Popular Hallertauer Hops

The major hop varieties grown today in Germany's biggest hop region.

Variety	Hectares	Variety	Hectares
Herkules	4,416	Spalter Select	444
Perle	2,821	Saphir	402
Tradition	2,800	Taurus	355
Magnum	1,591	Northern Brewer	155
Hersbrucker	948	Nugget	134
Hallertauer	533		
Other hops	848		

Figures relate to 2015. Source: Hopsteiner/International Hop Growers' Convention.

Who Owns Whom

Ownership of beer brands by multinational companies has become more complicated than ever. Below is a list of some of the world's best known beer brands and the international companies that (currently) own them.

Achouffe	Duvel Moortgat	Dreher (Hungary)	AB InBev*
Adelscott	Heineken	Dreher (Italy)	Heineken
Affligem	Heineken	Duckstein	Carlsberg
Aldaris	Carlsberg	Duvel	Duvel Moortgat
Amstel	Heineken	Edelweiss	Heineken
Ansells	Carlsberg	Faxe	Royal Unibrew
Baltika	Carlsberg	Feldschlössen	Carlsberg
Bass	AB InBev	Fischer	Heineken
Beamish	Heineken	Foster's (Europe)	Heineken
Beck's	AB InBev	Foster's (international)	AB InBev*
Belle-Vue	AB InBev	Franziskaner	AB InBev
Bintang	Heineken	Fürstenberg	Heineken
Blue Moon	Molson Coors	Gambrinus	AB InBev*
Boag's	Kirin	Giraf	Royal Unibrew
Boddingtons	AB InBev	Goose Island	AB InBev
Bohemia	AB InBev	Gösser	Heineken
Brahma	AB InBev	Gouden Boom	Bavaria
Budweiser	AB InBev	Grimbergen	Carlsberg
Caledonian	Heineken	Grolsch	Asahi*
Carling	Molson Coors	Guinness	Diageo
Carlsberg	Carlsberg	Hacker-Pschorr	Heineken
Castle	AB InBev*	Hahn	Kirin
Castlemaine XXXX	Kirin	Hansa	AB InBev*
Ceres	Royal Unibrew	Hapkin	Heineken
Ciney	Heineken	Harbin	AB InBev
Cobra	Molson Coors	Harp	Diageo
Coors	Molson Coors	Heineken	Heineken
Corona	Grupo Modelo	Henninger	Carlsberg
Cruzcampo	Heineken	Hertog Jan	AB InBev
De Koninck	Duvel Moortgat	Hoegaarden	AB InBev
Desperados	Heineken	Holsten	Carlsberg
Diebels	AB InBev	Hürlimann	Carlsberg
Dos Equis	Heineken	Jupiler	AB InBev

Kalnapilis	Royal Unibrew	Radegast	AB InBev*
Kanterbräu	Carlsberg	Ringnes	Carlsberg
Kilkenny	Diageo	Rodenbach	Bavaria
Kozel	AB InBev*	Rolling Rock	AB InBev
Kronenbourg	Carlsberg	Sagres	Heineken
Krusovice	Heineken	St Pauli Girl	AB InBev
Kulmbacher	Heineken	Sharp's	Molson Coors
Labatt's	AB InBev	Sinebrychoff	Carlsberg
Lapin Kulta	Heineken	Skol (Europe)	Carlsberg
Lech	AB InBev*	Skol (South America)	AB InBev
Leffe	AB InBev	John Smith's	Heineken
Leinenkugel's	AB InBev*	Snow	China Resources*
Liefmans	Duvel Moortgat	Sol	Heineken
Little Creatures	Kirin	Spaten	AB InBev
Löwenbräu	AB InBev	Speight's	Kirin
M&B	Molson Coors	Starobrno	Heineken
Mac's	Kirin	Staropramen	Molson Coors
Maes	Heineken	Steinlager	Kirin
Meantime	Asahi*	Stella Artois	AB InBev
Michelob	AB InBev	Stones	Molson Coors
Miller	AB InBev*	Super Bock	Carlsberg
Molson	Molson Coors	Svyturys	Carlsberg
Moretti	Heineken	Swan	Kirin
Mort Subite	Heineken	Tatra	Heineken
Murphy's	Heineken	Tecate	Heineken
Mythos	Carlsberg	Tetley's	Carlsberg
Newcastle Brown	Heineken	Tiger	Heineken
Okocim	Carlsberg	Toohey's	Kirin
Oranjeboom	AB InBev	Tuborg	Carlsberg
Palm	Bavaria	Tyskie	AB InBev*
Paulaner	Heineken†	Utenos	Carlsberg
Pelforth	Heineken	Vratislav	Molson Coors
Peroni	Asahi*	Warka	Heineken
Pilsner Urquell	AB InBev*	Wieckse Witte	Heineken
Poretti	Carlsberg	Worthington's	Molson Coors
Pripps	Carlsberg	Zipfer	Heineken
Quilmes	AB InBev	Zywiec	Heineken

* Pending finalisation of the AB InBev takeover of SABMiller. † Joint venture.

Some Ancient Hop Substitutes

Before hops became accepted as a standard brewing ingredient around five centuries ago, beer was often flavoured with other plants or herbs, spices and botanicals. Often these were combined into a mixture known as gruit. Below is a selection of the preferred choices of early brewers.

acorns	dandelion	mint
alecost	fennel seeds	mugwort
alehoof (ground ivy)	ginger	nettles
anise	heather	pepper
betony	horehound	sage
bog myrtle (sweet gale)	juniper	sweet flag
broom	laurel berries	tree bark
caraway	laurel leaves	wild rosemary
carrot seeds	lavender	woodruff
cinnamon	marjoram	wormwood
cumin	milk thistle	yarrow

The Biggest Round

Buying beer in rounds is a great British tradition and, it turns out, we're also the best in the world at it. On 15 June 2016, the record for the world's biggest round was smashed when Box Steam Brewery treated its customers to a free pint at the Cross Guns pub in Avoncliff, Wiltshire. Over a two-hour period, the brewery bought 412 drinks for customers to toast the 90th birthday of Queen Elizabeth II. The round included 283 pints – 35.4 imperial gallons – of Box Steam's Tunnel Vision ale and the effort broke the previous world record, set by country singer Merle Haggard in 1983 when he bought fans 5,095 one-ounce servings of whiskey (equivalent to 39.8 US gallons/33.14 imperial gallons) at a bar in Fort Worth, Texas.

CAMRA's Champion Bottled Beers

This contest, dedicated to bottle-conditioned beers, has been judged as part of CAMRA's Champion Beer of Britain awards every year since 1991.

1991	Worthington's White Shield (Bass)*
1992	Gale's Prize Old Ale
1993	Eldridge Pope Thomas Hardy's Ale
1994	Courage Imperial Russian Stout†
1995	King & Barnes Festive‡
1996	Marston's Oyster Stout†
1997	Hop Back Summer Lightning
1998	Fuller's 1845
1999	Young's Special London Ale
2000	Worthington's White Shield (King & Barnes)*
2001	RCH Ale Mary
2002	Fuller's 1845
2003	O'Hanlon's Original Port Stout
2004	Titanic Stout
2005	Durham Evensong
2006	Worthington's White Shield (Coors)*
2007	O'Hanlon's Original Port Stout
2008	Wye Valley Dorothy Goodbody's Wholesome Stout
2009	Titanic Stout
2010	St Austell Admiral's Ale
2011	St Austell Proper Job
2012	Stewart Embra
2013	Worthington's White Shield (Molson Coors)*
2014	Marble Chocolate Marble
2015	Harveys Imperial Extra Double Stout

* Beer changed brewery. † No longer bottle conditioned.

‡ No longer in production.

If You Can't Drink It, Eat It

The brewer's favourite cereal, barley, also lends its name to some of the world's most popular food dishes. The pasta shape 'macaroni' is actually derived from the Greek meaning 'food made from barley' and the word 'pasta' itself possibly comes from the Greek term for 'barley porridge'.

London Brewers' Alliance

In existence since 2010, the London Brewers' Alliance strives to promote excellence in all aspects of brewing within London. Its membership list – restricted to established commercial brewers within the loop of the M25 motorway (plus founder members, as previously agreed) – reflects how vibrant the brewing scene in the UK capital has become in recent years.

40FT Brewery
Alphabeta Brewery
Anspach & Hobday
Barnet Brewery
Beavertown
Beerblefish Brewing Co
Belleville Brewing Co
Bexley Brewery
Brew By Numbers
Brewhouse & Kitchen
Brick Brewery
Brightwater Brewery
Brixton Brewery
Brockley
Brodie Beers
Bullfinch Brewery
By The Horns Brewing Co
Camden Town Brewery
Canopy Beer Co
Clarkshaws
Crate
Cronx Brewery
Decent Brewery

Dragonfly Brewery
Earth Ale
East London Brewing Co
Enfield Brewery
Five Points Brewing Co
Four Pillars Brewery
Fourpure Brewing Co
Fuller's
Gipsy Hill Brewing Co
Hackney Brewery
Hammerton Brewery
Honest Brew
Hopstuff Brewery
Howling Hops
Kernel Brewery
Kew Brewery
The Laine Brewing Co
Late Knights Brewery
Left Bank Brewery
London Beer Factory
London Brewing Co
Meantime Brewing Co
Moncada Brewery

Mondo Brewing Co

One Mile End Brew Co

Orbit Brewing

The Park Brewery

Partizan Brewery

Portobello Brewery

Pressure Drop

Ram Brewery

Redchurch Brewery

Redemption

Reunion Ales

Rocky Head Brewery

Sambrook's

Signature Brewery

Solvay Society

Southwark Brewing Co

Tap East

TBH Essex Street Brewery

Thames Side Brewery

Truman's

Twickenham Fine Ales

UBREW

Volden

Weird Beard Brewing Co

Wild Card Brewery

Wimbledon Brewery

Windsor & Eton

Zerodegrees Blackheath

List includes full members brewing as of June 2016; the LBA also has a number of associate
member breweries, some of which are still in the planning stage.

Some Like It Stronger

Below is the average strength of beer as sold in a selection of countries.

Country	ABV	Country	ABV
Belgium	5.2%	Hungary	4.8%
Luxembourg	5.2%	Romania	4.8%
Canada	5.0%	Ukraine	4.8%
France	5.0%	Denmark	4.6%
Japan	5.0%	Finland	4.6%
Lithuania	5.0%	USA	4.6%
Netherlands	5.0%	Czech Republic	4.5%
Poland	5.0%	New Zealand	4.5%
Spain	5.0%	Slovakia	4.5%
Austria	4.9%	South Korea	4.5%
Italy	4.9%	Australia	4.3%
Bulgaria	4.8%	Ireland	4.3%
Germany	4.8%	UK	4.2%

Figures given are for 2013. Source: *British Beer & Pub Association Statistical Handbook 2015*.

Great British Beer Festival Venues

The Great British Beer Festival is the Campaign for Real Ale's big annual showcase of the best of British cask-conditioned ales with hundreds on sale, plus some of the best beers from overseas. Around 45,000 visitors attend during the course of the five-day event, which is held in the first or second week of August. The forerunner of the 'GBBF' was the Covent Garden Beer Festival, which was staged in London 9–13 September 1975.

1977–80	Alexandra Palace, London*
1981–2	Queens Hall, Leeds
1983	Bingley Hall, Birmingham
1984	No event
1985–7	Metropole Hotel, Brighton
1988–9	Queens Hall, Leeds
1990	Metropole Hotel, Brighton
1991	Docklands Arena, London
1992–2005	Olympia, London
2006–11	Earl's Court, London
2012–	Olympia, London

* 1980 event held in tents after Alexandra Palace fire.

A Beer with His Name On

How much do you love beer? Would it extend to naming one of your children after your favourite drink? That's what the brother of Oscar-winning actor Mathew McConaughey did when he decided to call his son Miller Lyte in honour of his regular tipple. It took the brewery nine years to discover this fact but, delighted with the publicity, it then sent the proud dad a year's supply of the brew. Maybe it's not such an odd story as strange names seem to run in the family. McConaughey's brother himself – although formally registered as Michael – for some reason likes to be known as Rooster. It is not known whether he has yet informed a certain North Yorkshire brewery in the hope of receiving further freebies.

What Are We Brewing?

The table below reveals the styles of beers produced most commonly by the UK's independent breweries. The percentages shown alongside relate to the number of breweries that now regularly produce each of the styles.

Pale golden bitter/golden ale	94.7%
Traditional brown/copper/amber bitter	83.4%
Stout/porter	74.4%
Strong bitter/IPA	67.4%
Traditional mild	30.6%
Strong mild/old ale	23.6%
Strong ale/barley wine	20.6%
Lager-style beer	20.6%
Wheat beer	14.3%
Gluten-free beer	1.7%
Lower alcohol beer (<2.8% ABV)	1.3%

Source: *British Beer* (SIBA member's survey 2016).

A Hop Tribute

Anyone who has seen the television detective series *Inspector Morse* – or read the original novels by Colin Dexter – can vouch for the hero's penchant for a pint of cask ale. Seldom could a case be cracked without a gallon or two of bitter to oil the cogs of the copper's brilliant brain. Morse became a hero to beer-lovers and his endorsement of their product was a boon for Britain's brewers during the 1980s. In 2013, the brewing industry repaid the compliment by naming a new hop after the slurping sleuth. The hop, a hybrid of Cascade and an unnamed hedgerow (dwarf) hop, was bred at Wye Hops in Kent and grown by Ali and Richard Capper on their farm on the Herefordshire/Worcestershire border. It was then released to Marston's for use in one of its Single Hop range of pale ales. Brewer Simon Yates named the hop (and the beer) Endeavour – Morse's mysterious first name, only revealed some ten years after the series began.

Twelve Really Unusual London Beer Venues

Not a conventional list of London's best pubs, but a selection (in purely alphabetical order) of a dozen of its most remarkable, unexpected, beer-friendly venues, compiled by beer educator and award-winning writer Des de Moor, author of *The CAMRA Guide to London's Best Beer, Pubs and Bars*.

1 Bean and Hop, 424 Garratt Lane SW18 4HN.
beanandhop.co.uk.
It looks like a trendy coffee shop but this Earlsfield shopfront houses one of the biggest bottled beer selections in the area, mainly from small London brewers. A sign of the times.

2 Blackfriar, 174 Queen Victoria Street EC4V 4EG.
nicholsons.co.uk
A place that has to be seen to be believed: a gobsmacking early 20th-century art nouveau riot of stained glass, multi-coloured marble and bas-reliefs with fanciful depictions of monastic life.

3 Dalston Eastern Curve Garden Café, 13 Dalston Lane E8 3DF.
dalstongarden.org
An exquisite, enclosed community garden on a disused rail line provides perhaps London's most beautiful beery setting. 40FT Brewery, just around the corner in a recycled shipping container, is noteworthy, too.

4 Euston Tap, West Lodge, 190 Euston Road NW1 2EF.
eustontap.com
A specialist beer bar in one of the neoclassical lodges that once flanked Euston's demolished Doric Arch, making great use of the restricted space.

5 Howling Hops Tank Bar, 9 Queens Yard E9 5EN.
howlinghops.co.uk
Post-industrial venue in a converted factory at Hackney Wick dispensing ten house-brewed beers direct from the maturation vessels. Bottles, too.

6 Leyton Orient Supporters Club, Matchroom Stadium,
Oliver Road E10 5NF. orientsupporters.org
Top-class cask and bottled beers served at a friendly, volunteer-run football stadium bar, though you'll need to check the opening times and

present a CAMRA/EBCU card if you are not a member. If closed, try the Leyton Technical in a lavish former town hall and college just up the road.

7 **Mahogany Bar**, Graces Alley E1 8JB. wiltons.org.uk
Sample from a well-chosen beer range in the atmospheric surroundings of a surviving Victorian music hall in the East End.

8 **One Inn The Wood**, 209 Petts Wood Road BR5 1LA.
oneinnthewood.co.uk
One of the new breed of micropubs where you can now enjoy gravity-poured local cask beers in suburban shopping parades.

9 **Parcel Yard**, King's Cross Station N1C 4AH.
parcelyard.co.uk
A derelict Grade I-listed railway parcels building transformed as part of the King's Cross regeneration scheme into a vast Fuller's pub that puts the usual dull station bars to shame.

10 **Tap East**, Great Eastern Market, Westfield, Stratford City E20 1ET.
tapeast.co.uk
A serious specialist beer bar in a mega-mall alongside the Olympic Park and opposite Stratford International station? Yes, thanks to the team behind Borough Market's legendary Rake bar.

11 **Understudy**, National Theatre, Southbank SE1 9PX.
nationaltheatre.org.uk
This excellent beer bar in the corner of the brutalist landmark the National Theatre was amazingly the first catering outlet in the building to make something of its riverside setting.

12 **Wanstead Tap**, 352 Winchelsea Road E7 0AQ.
thewansteadtap.com
In a railway arch, amid car repair shops, just around the corner from Wanstead Flats, this is a community space, performance venue, cinema and top-notch beer bar and bottle shop.

Brand Extensions

Sometimes brewers can't get enough of a successful brand, so they spin-off another beer or two in the hope that the sales just keep rolling in.

Brand	Extension(s)
Beck's	Beck's Vier
Budweiser	Bud Lite
Brains SA	SA Gold
Brains The Rev James	The Rev James Gold/Rye
Duvel	Duvel Triple Hop
Foster's	Foster's Gold/Twist
Greene King Abbot Ale	Abbot Reserve
Greene King IPA	IPA Gold/IPA Reserve
Greene King Old Speckled Hen	Old Hoppy Hen/Old Golden Hen/ Old Crafty Hen/Old Spirited Hen
Hoegaarden	Hoegaarden Rosée
Kronenbourg 1664	Kronenbourg 1664 Blanc
Marston's Pedigree	Pedigree New World Pale Ale
Miller	Miller Lite
Shepherd Neame Spitfire	Spitfire Gold
Stella Artois	Stella 4%/Stella Black
Vedett	Vedett Extra White/Vedett Extra IPA

The US Craft Brewing Boom

Year	Craft Breweries	Market Share*
2011	1,977	5.7%
2012	2,401	6.5%
2013	2,863	7.8%
2014	3,676	11.0%
2015	4,225	12.2%

* By volume. Source: Brewers Association.

Beer Gods and Goddesses

Beer has been important to humanity for millennia as is evident from the numerous gods and goddess of beer that have been worshipped around the world. Some share their beer duties with other areas of patronage, such as fertility and the harvest, but here are some of the most prominent.

Aegir
The Norse god of the sea was also the brewer of the best beer.

Mamlambo
A Zulu river goddess who also looked after the women who made beer.

Mbaba Mwanna Waresa
A Zulu fertility goddess who, it is said, invented beer and taught people to brew.

Ninkasi
Possibly the best-known beer deity: a Sumerian goddess worshipped in a hymn found on an ancient clay tablet that reveals how beer was brewed 4,000 years ago.

Ragutis
A Lithuanian god assisted by his wife, Ragutiene, in the role of local beer deities.

Silenus
A Greek god, companion and tutor to the more familiar Dionysus.

Dark Vision

Back in December 1759, one of the shrewdest business deals of all time was struck when a 34-year-old entrepreneur named Arthur Guinness took a 9,000-year lease on a four-acre property in Dublin. Rainsford's Ale Brewery was a struggling business and it was, therefore, somewhat of a risky move for the ambitious young brewer to acquire the site but he turned it to his advantage, building up a global business for his porters and stouts. And the terms of the lease? Well, £45 a year may have seemed a lot at the time but it proved to be quite a bargain, although that's not what the company pays today because it purchased the land (and more) outright many years ago.

The Independent Family Brewers of Britain

The Independent Family Brewers of Britain (IFBB) is an association of surviving family brewers, founded in 1993 to promote and protect the historic and community values of the UK's independent breweries, the pubs they operate and the beers they produce. Member companies are:

Arkell's Brewery Ltd
George Bateman & Son Ltd
WH Brakspear & Sons Ltd*
Black Sheep Brewery plc
Daniel Batham & Son Ltd
SA Brain & Co Ltd
Donnington Brewery
Everards Brewery Ltd
Fuller, Smith & Turner plc
Hall & Woodhouse Ltd
Harvey & Son (Lewes) Ltd
Holden's Brewery Ltd
Joseph Holt Ltd
Hook Norton Brewery Co Ltd

Hydes Brewery Ltd
JW Lees & Co Brewers Ltd
McMullen & Sons Ltd
Palmers Brewery
Frederic Robinson Ltd
St Austell Brewery Co Ltd
Shepherd Neame Ltd
Timothy Taylor & Co Ltd
T&R Theakston Ltd
Daniel Thwaites plc
Titanic Brewery Ltd
Wadworth & Co Ltd
Charles Wells Ltd
Young & Co's Brewery plc*

* Now a pub company.

Some Completely Organic British Breweries

Atlantic, Treisaac, Cornwall
Black Isle, Munlochy, Highland
Boudicca, Norwich, Norfolk
Butts, Great Shefford, Berkshire
Laverstoke Park Farm, Overton, Hampshire*
Liverpool Organic, Liverpool, Merseyside
Melbourn Bros, Stamford, Lincolnshire
Pitfield, North Weald, Essex

* Beers contract brewed for the farm.

At some other breweries, such as Little Valley in Yorkshire and Stroud in Gloucestershire, much of the output is organic. Also, many more produce at least one organic beer.

Capital Beer: Berlin

Five pubs and bars well worth a visit on a stay in Germany's capital city.

Alt-Berliner Weissbierstubl, Rathausstrasse 21, 10178
Central pub-restaurant in old style. As its name suggests, a good place to try the local Berliner weissbier, if only from a bottle.

Georgebräu, Spreeufer 4, 10178
Huge brew pub with many rooms and a terrace that overlooks the river.

Hops and Barley, Wühlischstrasse 22/23, 10245
Popular, two-room brew pub on the east side, serving its own organic beers. Popular with football fans.

Prater Garden, Kastanienallee 7–9, 10435
Former ballroom, theatre and meeting place, reinvented as a pub-restaurant in the 1990s, with a beer garden – the oldest in town – seating 600.

Vagabund Brauerei, Antwerpener Strasse 3, 13353
Brew pub set up by three American friends in the Wedding district, north-west of the city.

Beer for a Butterfly

One way to enjoy a free drink is to take part in the Beer for a Butterfly contest held in California every year. The competition has been organised by Professor Art Shapiro of the University of California, Davis, since 1972. The professor records the date the first cabbage white butterfly of the year is trapped, to help his research into climate change, and whoever catches that first butterfly is treated to a pitcher of beer. But, before you rush off to the West Coast, just bear in mind one thing: you'll have to be extremely quick off the mark to claim the prize. Professor Shapiro has won the contest himself on all but three occasions.

Some Celebrities Who Have Advertised Beer

Celebrity	Beer
Jessica Alba	Tiger Beer
Jennifer Aniston	Heineken
Armstrong & Miller	Shepherd Neame Spitfire
Gina Bellman	Boddingtons
Victor Borge	Heineken
Susan Boyle	Yebisu
Eric Cantona	Kronenbourg 1664
Anna Chancellor	Boddingtons
Chas & Dave	Courage Best
George Clooney	Kirin
James Coburn	Schlitz Light
Billy Connolly	Kaliber
Peter Cook	Watney's Brown
Peter Cook & Dudley Moore	Guinness
Daniel Craig	Heineken
Lawrence Dallaglio	Greene King IPA
Paul Daniels & Debbie McGee	Heineken
Jack Dee	John Smith's
Douglas Fairbanks, Jnr & Gertrude Lawrence	Whitbread Pale Ale
Vanessa Feltz	Heineken
Will Ferrell	Old Milwaukee
Bryan Ferry	Carlsberg
Andrew Flintoff	Thwaites Lancaster Bomber
Harrison Ford	Kirin
Nick Hancock	Randalls
Rutger Hauer	Guinness
Jimmy Hill	Heineken
Paris Hilton	Devassa
Paul Hogan	Foster's
Engelbert Humperdinck	John Smith's
Griff Rhys Jones	Holsten Pils
Peter Kay	John Smith's
Anna Kendrick	Newcastle Brown Ale
Lucy Liu	Suntory Diet Beer
Lawrie McMenemy	Barbican
Mr Magoo	Stag
James May	Fuller's London Pride
Rik Mayall	Wells Bombardier
Bernard Miles	Mackeson
Bob Mortimer	Wells Bombardier
Sarah Parish	Boddingtons
Brad Pitt	Heineken
Lionel Richie	Tap King
Lisa Riley	Heineken
Jonathan Ross	Harp
Stevan Seagal	Carlton Dry
Peter Stringfellow	Heineken
Patrick Swayze	Pabst Blue Ribbon
Melanie Sykes	Boddingtons
Holly Valance	Foster's Gold
Jean-Claude Van Damme	Coors Light
Orson Welles	Carlsberg
Ray Winstone	Holsten

How to Use a Swan Neck and Sparkler

Many pubs are fitted with swan neck dispense systems for cask ale. The concept was created to generate a thick, creamy head on a pint but it can only achieve this if a sparkler nozzle is fitted to the end and the appropriate procedure, as outlined below, is followed. Note, however, that many beers, particularly those brewed in southern England, which are not meant to have a deep head of foam, should not be dispensed in this way (the breweries section of the *Good Beer Guide* provides dispense advice for each brewery's beers). For those beers, the sparkler should be removed and the beer should be poured with the swan neck pipe out of the glass.

1	2	3	4	5
Sparkler on BOTTOM of empty glass	Use good, steady initial pull	Essential to keep sparkler IN beer	At finish of dispense, top up keeping sparkler UNDER beer head	**PERFECT PINT!**

Diagram published in the *Marston's Cask Ale Report 2013*.

Beer, Birds and Books

In the early 1950s, an argument between participants at a game shoot had an unexpected upside – it led to the creation of one of the world's biggest-selling publications. The dispute, over the fastest game bird in Europe, was waged between Sir Hugh Beaver, then managing director of Guinness, and other guests at the event in County Wexford, Ireland. As no one could provide a definitive answer, and existing reference books could not resolve the query, Beaver decided to commission his own book of facts that could also be used as a marketing vehicle for his beer. The result was the *Guinness Book of Records*, compiled by twins Norris and Ross McWhirter. From the first edition, published in 1955, it was a huge hit.

Major Beer Festivals Worldwide

Location	Festival	Month
Australia		
Melbourne/ Sydney	Great Australian Beer Spectapular	May
Belgium		
Leuven	Zythos Beer Fest	April
Buggenhout	Weekend of Spontaneous Fermentation	May
Eizeringen	Day of the Kriek	June
Olen	Weekend of Belgian Beers	June
Brussels	Belgian Beer Weekend	September
Poperinge	Poperinge Beer Festival	October
Essen	Christmas Beer Festival	December
Brazil		
Blumenau	Festival Brasileira da Cerveja	March
Canada		
Montreal	Mondial de la Bière	June
Victoria	Great Canadian Beer Festival	September
China		
Hong Kong	Beertopia	November
Czech Republic		
Prague	Czech Beer Festival	May
Denmark		
Copenhagen	Copenhagen Beer Festival	May
France		
Mulhouse	Mondial de la Bière Europe	February
Germany		
Berlin	Berlin International Beer Festival	August
Munich	Oktoberfest	September
Japan		
Okinawa/ Yokohama	Great Japan Beer Festival	April
Tokyo	Great Japan Beer Festival	June
Osaka/Nagoya	Great Japan Beer Festival	July
Yokohama	Great Japan Beer Festival	September
Latvia		
Riga	Latviabeerfest	May

Greece
Corfu .... Corfu Beer Festival .... October
Italy
Rome .... Fermentazioni .... September
Netherlands
Oisterwijk .... Biermatinee .... July
Amsterdam .... Pint Bokbierfestival .... October
New Zealand
Christchurch .... The Great Kiwi Beer Festival .... January
Wellington .... Beervana .... August
Singapore
Singapore .... Beerfest Asia .... June
Poland
Warsaw .... Warsaw Beer Festival .... April
Spain
Barcelona .... Barcelona Beer Festival .... March
Serbia
Belgrade .... Belgrade Beer Festival .... August
Sweden
Söderbärke .... SMÖF Microbrewery Festival .... October
Stockholm .... Stockholm Beer and Whisky Festival ..... October
UK
Varies .... National Winter Ales Festival .... January
Manchester .... Manchester Beer & Cider Festival .... January
London .... Craft Beer Rising .... February
London .... London Drinker .... March
Sheffield .... Beer X .... March
Cambridge .... Cambridge Beer Festival .... May
Edinburgh .... Scottish Real Ale Festival .... July
London .... Great British Beer Festival .... August
Peterborough .... Peterborough Beer Festival .... August
Cardiff .... Great Welsh Beer & Cider Festival .... September
Manchester .... Indy Man Beer Con .... October
USA
Portland (Oregon) ... Spring Beer & Wine Festival .... March
South Boston .... New England Real Ale Exhibition .... April
  (Massachusetts)   (NERAX)
Denver (Colorado) ... Great American Beer Festival .... October
Durham (N Carolina) ...World Beer Festival .... October

The European Beer Consumers Union

The European Beer Consumers Union (EBCU) was founded in 1990. It is a federation of national beer consumer groups whose objectives are the promotion of Europe's beer culture and traditional beer styles, as well as championing diversity and consumer choice, enhancing the image of beer and representing consumers' interests. These are current members.

Austria: *BierIG*	bierig.org
Belgium: *Zythos*	zythos.be
Czech Republic: *Sdružení Přátel Piva*	pratelepiva.cz
Denmark: *Danske Ølentusiaster*	ale.dk
Finland: *Olutliitto*	olutliitto.fi
Ireland: *Beoir*	beoir.org
Italy: *Unionbirrai*	unionbirrai.com
MoBI	movimentobirra.it
Netherlands: *PINT*	pint.nl
Norway: *NORØL*	nor-ale.org
Poland: *Bractwo Piwne*	bractwopiwne.pl
Sweden: *Svenska Ölfrämjandet*	svenskaolframjandet.se
Switzerland: *L'Association des Buveurs d'Orges*	abo-ch.org
UK: *CAMRA*	camra.org.uk

UK Breweries Still Employing Coopers

A cooper is a maker and repairer of wooden casks, a position that has been lost at nearly all breweries since the arrival of metal containers. In addition to the three breweries mentioned below, other breweries also occasionally offer some 'beer from the wood' but do not employ a cooper.

Brewery	*Cooper*
Marston's*	Mark Newton
Samuel Smith	David Poulter
Theakston	Jonathan Manby

* Not for casks used for delivery but just for the upkeep of the wooden casks used in the Burton Union fermentation system.

CAMRA's National Clubs of the Year

1986	ICI Recreation Club, Huddersfield, West Yorkshire
1987–8	West Herts Social Club, Watford, Hertfordshire
1989	St Teresa's Parish Social Centre, Pentworth, Lancashire
1990	No event
1991	ICI Recreation Club, Huddersfield, West Yorkshire
1992	No event
1993	Galleywood Social Club, Galleywood, Essex
1994–5	Appleton Thorne Village Hall, Warrington, Cheshire
1996	No event
1997	Howerd Club, Eltham, London
1998	Ouse Amateur Sailing Club, Ouse, Norfolk
1999	Wakefield Labour Club, Wakefield, West Yorkshire/ Rushden Historical Transport Society Club, Rushden, Northamptonshire (joint)
2000–2	Somer's Sports and Social Club, Halesowen, West Midlands
2003	No event
2004	Sebastopol Social Club, Sebastopol, Torfaen, Wales
2005	Hastings Club, Lytham St Anne's, Lancashire
2006	Dartford Working Men's Club, Dartford, Kent
2007	Greetland Community & Sporting Association, Halifax, West Yorkshire
2008	Leyton Orient Supporters Club, London/Appleton Thorn Village Hall, Warrington, Cheshire (joint)
2009	Guiseley Factory Workers Club, Guiseley, West Yorkshire
2010	Rushden Historical Transport Society Club, Rushden, Northamptonshire
2011	Kinver Constitutional Club, Kinver, Staffordshire
2012	Questors Grapevine Club, Ealing, London
2013	Cheltenham Motor Club, Cheltenham, Gloucestershire
2014	Barnton Cricket Club, Northwich, Cheshire
2015	Wortley Men's Club, Wortley, South Yorkshire
2016	Albatross RAFA Club, Bexhill, East Sussex

Although the contest has run continuously, the judging procedure has occasionally extended over more than one calendar year, and a winner has not been announced every year.

Britain's Most Consistently Good Beers

The following table features beers that have been consistent category finalists in CAMRA's Champion Beer of Britain and Champion Winter Beer of Britain competitions in recent years. Many have not gone on to win any titles but nevertheless they deserve recognition for their consistent quality.

Beer	Times Finalist*
Milds	
Rudgate Ruby Mild†	3
Triple fff Pressed Rat & Warthog	3
Williams Bros Black†	3
Bitters	
Acorn Barnsley Bitter	5
Hawkshead Bitter	4
Salopian Shropshire Gold	4
Timothy Taylor Boltmaker†	4
Buntingford Twitchell†	3
Purity Pure Gold	3
Best Bitters	
Surrey Hills Shere Drop†	5
Bank Top Flat Cap	3
Bathams Best Bitter	3
Green Jack Trawlerboys Best Bitter†	3
Purple Moose Glaslyn Ale	3
Salopian Darwin's Origin†	3
Strong Bitters	
Salopian Golden Thread	3
Old Ales and Strong Milds	
Adnams Old Ale	3
Beowulf Dark Raven	3
Leeds Midnight Bell	3
Palmers Tally Ho!	3
Purple Moose Dark Side of the Moose†	3

Beer	Times Finalist*
Golden Ales	
Fyne Jarl†	3
Salopian Oracle	3
Porters	
Elland 1872 Porter†	4
Ayr Rabbie's Porter	3
Blythe Johnsons	3
RCH Old Slug Porter	3
Stouts	
Heart of Wales Welsh Black	4
Ascot Anastasia's Exile Stout	3
Cairngorm Black Gold†	3
Titanic Stout	3
Barley Wines and Strong Ales	
Kinver Over the Edge†	5
Darwin Extinction Ale†	4
Heart of Wales High as a Kite	3
Moor Old Freddy Walker	3
Speciality Beers	
Saltaire Triple Chocoholic†	4
Bottled Beers	
Fuller's 1845	4
Marble Chocolate Marble†	3
Marble Lagonda IPA	3
Molson Coors Worthington's White Shield†	3
O'Hanlon's Original Port Stout	3
St Austell Proper Job	3
Stewart Embra†	3

* 2012–16 (2011–15 for bottled beers) † Category winner on at least one occasion.

A Recipe for Staying Sober

Samuel Adams beer founder Jim Koch claims to have found a way to help himself stay sober during a drinking session. Through a conversation with a microbiologist friend, Koch came up with the novel idea of mixing a teaspoonful of dried baker's yeast into some yoghurt and eating this before enjoying a few beers. While not eradicating the effects of drinking, Koch says, it can mitigate them because an enzyme in the yeast reacts with the alcohol in the beer, breaking it down before it enters the bloodstream. Scientists remain cautious, however, one questioning how the yeast enzyme could survive the intensity of stomach acid and also suggesting that byproducts created during the breakdown of alcohol could actually make hangovers worse. Others claim that the effects will differ from person to person and suggest that simply having some food or water in the stomach before drinking is equally or even more effective.

Pub Diplomacy

When a foreign statesman is in town, British prime ministers understand that the best place to make an impression is in the pub. In 1994, John Major famously once treated Russian president Boris Yeltsin to a pint at the Bernard Arms, Great Kimble, close to Chequers, the PM's country retreat in Buckinghamshire, although they did have to wait for the pub to open up specially before quenching their thirst. The same pub had once been frequented by Harold Wilson, just before his resignation in 1976. In 2003, Tony Blair wowed teetotal US President George W Bush at the Dun Cow at Sedgefield (Blair's parliamentary constituency), then, in 2015, David Cameron followed suit by introducing Chinese premier Xi Jinping to traditional British ale at the Plough, Cadsden (again close to Chequers). This was the same pub where a somewhat embarrassed Cameron had inadvertently left his young daughter after a family lunch three years previously.

Open-Source Brewing

In an extension of the spirit of collaboration that pervades the modern brewing industry, prominent Scottish brewery BrewDog has made all its beer recipes available to the general public. The DIY Dog scheme reveals the secrets behind more than 200 beers brewed by the company since its founding in 2005 – from the ingredients (with quantities) to mash and fermentation temperatures – encouraging home brewers to try and recreate their favourites or add a new spin to a familiar BrewDog beer.

Craft Brewery Takeovers

Some of the new, smaller breweries acquired by big brewing companies in recent times as they attempt to grab a slice of the 'craft beer' action.

Brewery (Country)	Buyer	Year
10 Barrel (US)	AB InBev	2014
Achouffe (Belgium)	Duvel Moortgat	2006
Baden Baden (Brazil)	Schincariol*	2007
Ballast Point (US)	Constellation Brands	2015
Birra del Borgo (Italy)	AB InBev	2016
Blue Point (US)	AB InBev	2014
Bogotá Beer (Colombia)	AB InBev	2015
Boulevard (US)	Duvel Moortgat	2013
Breckenridge (US)	AB InBev	2015
Camden Town (UK)	AB InBev	2015
Colorado (Brazil)	AB InBev	2015
Cricketers Arms (Australia)	Asahi	2013
Devils Backbone (US)	AB InBev	2016
Eisenbahn (Brazil)	Schincariol*	2008
Elysian (US)	AB InBev	2015
Fordham (US)	AB InBev†	2007
Founders (US)	Mahou San Miguel†	2014
Four Peaks (US)	AB InBev	2015
Franciscan Well (Ireland)	Molson Coors	2013
Golden Road (US)	AB InBev	2015
Goose Island (US)	AB InBev	2011
Hop Valley	MillerCoors	2016

Lagunitas (US)	Heineken (50%)	2015
Little Creatures (Australia)	Lion Nathan*	2012
Magic Hat (US)	North American Breweries‡	2010
Matilda Bay (Australia)	Foster's§	1990
McCashin's (New Zealand)	Lion Nathan*	1999
Meantime (UK)	SABMiller‖	2015
Mendocino (US)	United Breweries	1997
Mountain Goat (Australia)	Asahi	2015
Ommegang (US)	Duvel Moortgat	2005
Pyramid (US)	North American Breweries‡	2010
Redhook (US)	Anheuser-Busch¶	1994
Saint Archer (US)	MillerCoors#	2015
Sharp's (UK)	Molson Coors	2011
Terrapin (US)	MillerCoors#	2016
Wäls (Brazil)	AB InBev	2015

* Now part of Kirin. † Minority shareholding. ‡ Now part of FIFCO (Costa Rica).
§ Now part of AB InBev. ‖ Now to be part of Asahi (pending finalisation of the AB InBev takeover of SABMiller). ¶ Now part of Craft Brew Alliance – 32%-owned by AB InBev – that also includes Widmer Brothers and Kona (US). # Now operating as Molson Coors.

Time Travel in Denmark

Back in 1883, Carlsberg gave the world the first pure yeast strain for lager production. Previously, brewers had used yeast that was made up of various strains, some of which turned beer bad. Scientist Emil Christian Hansen solved the problem in the Carlsberg laboratory by isolating the best strain. When, a few years ago, the Danish company discovered some bottles of beer dating from that very same year in its Copenhagen cellars, it sensed an opportunity. Skilfully, yeast found in the bottles was cultivated back to fighting fitness and used to produce as near a replica of that original 'pure' beer as possible. In 2016, a select group of dignitaries – including Denmark's Crown Prince – were the first to sample beer as it might have tasted 133 years before.

The Brewers of Europe

The Brewers of Europe is a European-wide trade organisation with 26 members (from within the EU) and three associate members. It was founded in 1958 and works to promote and protect the interests of Europe's brewing industry. The offices of the association are located at: Rue Caroly 23–25, 1050 Brussels, Belgium; www.brewersofeurope.org.

Austria: *Bierland Österreich* bierserver.at
    Zaunergasse 1–3, A-1030 Vienna
Belgium: *Belgian Brewers* belgianbrewers.be
    Maison des Brasseurs, Grand'Place 10, B-1000 Brussels
Bulgaria: *UBB – Union of Brewers in Bulgaria* pivovari.com
    16 Bacho Kiro Street, 1000 Sofia
Croatia: *Croatian Chamber of Commerce* hgk.hr
    Association of Beer, Malt and Hop Producers
    Rooseveltov trg 2, 10000 Zagreb
Cyprus: *Cyprus Brewers Association*
    PO Box 21455, 1509 Nicosia
Czech Republic: *Czech Beer and Malt Association* ceske-pivo.cz
    Lipova 15, 120 44 Praha, 2
Denmark: *Bryggeriforeningen* bryggeriforeningen.dk
    Faxehus, Gamle Carlsberg Vej 16, 1900 Copenhagen V
Finland: *Panimoliitto – Finnish Federation of the Brewing Industry*
    panimoliitto.fi Pasilankatu 2, PO Box 115, 00241 Helsinki
France: *Brasseurs de France* brasseurs-de-france.com
    Boulevard Malesherbes 9, F-75008 Paris
Germany: *Deutscher Brauer-Bund e.V.* brauer-bund.de
    Neustädtische Kirchstrasse 7a, 10117 Berlin
Greece: *Greek Brewers' Association*
    107 Kifissou Ave, 122 41 Egaleo
Hungary: *Association of Hungarian Brewers* sorszovetseg.hu
    Margitsziget Grand Hotel, 4th Floor, 1138-Budapest
Ireland: *The Irish Brewers' Association* abfi.ie
    Confederation House, 84–86 Lower Baggot Street, Dublin 2
Italy: *Assobirra – Associazione degli Industriali della Birra e del Malto*
    assobirra.it Via Giuseppe Pisanelli 1, 00196 Rome

Lithuania: *Lithuanian Brewers Guild*   aludariai.lt
  A Tuméno g.4, 01109 Vilnius
Luxembourg: *Féderation des Brasseurs Luxembourgeois*
  Rue Alcide de Gaspéri, 7, BP 1304, L-1013 Luxembourg-Kirchberg
Malta: *Malta Federation of Industry*
  Casa Leone, Pjazza Robert Zamut, Floriana FRN 1119
Netherlands: *Nederlandse Brouwers*   nederlandsebrouwers.nl
  Dagelijkse Groenmarkt 3–5, 2513 AL Den Haag
Norway: *Brewery and Beverage Association**   bryggeriforeningen.no
  Sorkedalsveien 6, PO Box 7087 Majorstuen, 0306 Oslo
Poland: *Browary Polskie*   browary-polskie.pl
  Biuro Zarzadu Zwiazku, Al. Jana Pawla II 12 lok. 339, 00-124 Warsaw
Portugal: *APCV – Associação Portuguesa dos Produtores de Cerveja*
  apcv.pt   Edificio EE3, Pólo Tecnológico de Lisboa, Lote 3,
  1600-546 Lisbon
Romania: *Brewers of Romania Association*   berariiromaniei.ro
  Modern Business Center, Bdul Carol 1 34–36, Bucharest 020922
Slovakia: *Slovak Beer and Malt Association*   slovenskepivo.sk
  Zahradnicka 21, 811 07 Bratislava
Slovenia: *Brewing Association of Slovenia*
  Pivovarniška Ulica 2, 1000 Ljubljana
Spain: *Cerveceros de España*   cerveceros.org
  Almagro 24 – 2° Izda., 28010 Madrid
Sweden: *Sveriges Bryggerier AB*   sverigesbryggerier.se
  Kungsgatan 35, 114 56 Stockholm
Switzerland: *Swiss Breweries Federation**   bier.ch
  Enqimattstrasse 11, PO Box 2124, CH-8027 Zürich
Turkey: *Beer and Malt Producers' Association (BMÜD)**   biramalt.com
  Tunus Caddesi 8/15, Kavaklidere Ankara
UK: *British Beer & Pub Association*   beerandpub.com
  Ground Floor, Brewers' Hall, Aldermanbury Square,
  London EC2V 7HR

* Associate member.

The Lambic Brewers

Only eight breweries (listed below) still produce traditional (or 'oud') lambic beer – the spontaneously fermented 'wild' beer of Belgium – although other companies – De Cam, Hanssens, Oud Beersel and Tilquin – use their products for blending, or for steeping with cherries and other fruit. Other Belgian businesses like De Ranke, Dilewyns and Kerkom blend the lambics with other ales to produce 'versnijsbier' (literally 'cut beer').

Boon	Girardin
Cantillon	Lindemans
De Troch	Mort Subite (Heineken)
Drie Fonteinen	Timmermans

Top Pressure

Talk to veteran CAMRA members and you'll still occasionally hear them discussing top pressure. They speak of it as if it were an evil that haunted their youth, and to an extent it was. In the early days of CAMRA, along with the struggle against brewery takeovers that were restricting choice for drinkers and the perils of fizzy, tasteless, pasteurised keg beer that was being foisted on customers in place of traditionally brewed beer, top pressure was way up there as a target. Essentially, top pressure was the rather stupid practice of taking a perfectly good, traditionally-brewed cask ale and ruining at the point of dispense by forcing it to the bar with carbon dioxide, instead of using a simple handpump. The beer may not have been pasteurised but its character was instantly changed for the worse by this heavy injection of gas. Breweries in the first *Good Beer Guide* were castigated for their use of the practice. 'Often spoilt by pressurisation', it remarked about Felinfoel in Llanelli, Wales; 'Good ale, often ruined by pressure' was the comment on Hydes of Manchester; 'Good when it's not gassed up' was the summary of Shepherd Neame's efforts. Thankfully, this is one frustrating aspect of pub life that seems to have quietly faded away.

British Beer Exports

	Country	Thousand hl
1	Ireland	1,250.5
2	USA	1,088.7
3	France	716.8
4	Netherlands	436.7
5	Italy	360.0
6	Belgium & Luxembourg	240.8
7	Canada	236.3
8	Sweden	108.0
9	Australasia	73.5
10	Spain	72.0
11	Russia	63.2
12	Germany	57.0
13	Cyprus	32.2
14	Finland	23.4
15	Norway	21.7
16	Poland	21.6
17	Denmark	14.4
18	Switzerland	12.3
19	Greece	9.9
20	Austria	7.3
	Other countries	395.6

Figures given are for 2014.

Source: *British Beer & Pub Association Statistical Handbook 2015*.

Pubs with Two Names

The White Horse at Prior's Dean, Hampshire, is a little tricky to find, not least because it has long been known to locals as the 'Pub With No Name', because of the marked absence of a pub sign. Even the pub's website – pubwithnoname.co.uk – plays along. As if to make up for this shortcoming, at least two pubs elsewhere in Britain somewhat greedily now have more than one name, as verified by the signage outside. If you pay a visit to the Railway Inn, aka the Dust Hole, in Salisbury or to the Gardeners Arms/ Murderers in the centre of Norwich, you'll see how confusing this can be.

The Cask Ale Drinker at a Glance

The typical British cask ale drinker can apparently be described as follows.

Age:		Gender:	
18–24	11%	Male	83%
25–34	18%	Female	17%
35–44	19%		
45–54	20%	Social Grade:	
55+	32%	ABC1	61%
		C2DE	39%

Source: *The Cask Report 2015–16*.

The Origins of Unusual British Brewery Names

Brewery	Origin
1648	Year King Charles I deposed
360°	Greenwich meridian
40FT	Length of shipping-container home
8 Sail	Windmill
Baltic Fleet	Home pub
Bishop Nick	Nicholas Ridley, Bishop of London
Campervan	Brews in a campervan
Concrete Cow	Local sculptures
Cotswold Lion	Breed of sheep
Cronx	Amalgam of Croydon and Bronx
Dancing Men	Sherlock Holmes story
Derventio	Roman town in the Midlands
Deva Craft	Roman name for Chester
Exit 33	Junction on M1 motorway
FILO	Home pub name (First In Last Out)
Flack Manor	WWII aircrew recuperation centre
Four Candles	*Two Ronnies* sketch
Golden Triangle	Area of Norwich
Goldstone	20-ton rock
Kernel	Barleycorns (kernels)
Left Handed Giant	Legendary Bristol figure
Long Man	Local chalk figure

Longdog	Pet lurcher
Meantime	Greenwich meridian
Nelson	Chatham historic dockyard
Newby Wyke	A Hull trawler
Old Bog	Housed in converted toilets
Old Spot	Sheepdog
Opa Hay's	Brewer's great grandfather
Philsters	Brewer's nickname
Pig Iron	Based on former ironworks
Platform 5	Beneath Newton Abbot station
Problem Child	Family history
S&P	Former brewery Steward & Patteson
Scribbler's	One partner an author
Sonnet 43	Elizabeth Barrett Browning poem
Steel City	Location in Sheffield
Summer Wine	Local *Last of the Summer Wine* filming
Tombstone	Original proximity to cemetery
Triple fff	Musical notation for *fortissimo* (very loud)
Two Towers	Birmingham landmarks
Verulam	Roman name for St Albans
Whittington's	Dick Whittington was local
Wooden Hand	One-handed local pirate
Woodforde's	18th-century parson
Wooha	Young son's exclamation
Zerodegrees	Greenwich meridian

Branded 'Craft' Beer Bar Chains in the UK

Chain	Outlets
BrewDog	27
Brewhouse & Kitchen	15
Draft House	9
Craft Beer Co.	7
North Bar	6
Zerodegrees	4

Figures correct as of August 2016.

Some of these companies also operate pubs and bars under different names.

Beer and Food Pairing, Vegetarian Style

It's not just meat and fish that beer complements so well, as is proved by this showcase vegetarian dinner prepared by Salon restaurant, Brixton, London, in August 2016 for the US Brewers Association, which supplied all the American beers (offering a selection of two beers for each course).

Courgette Tempura, Kirsch Beer Vinaigrette
Dehydrated Tomato, Yogurt, Sourdough Crisp
Radishes, Roasted Yeast
served with
Empire Brewing Skinny Atlas Light
Victory Brewing Kirsch Gose

***

Marinated Beetroots, Whipped Sheep's Curd, Puffed Barley, Hibiscus
served with
New Holland Brewing Full Circle
Great Divide Brewing Nadia Kali Hibiscus Saison

***

Girolles, Sweetcorn, Orange, Allspice Butter
served with
Hardywood Park Craft Brewery The Great Return
Sierra Nevada Brewing Torpedo

***

Smoked Celeriac Steak, Rainbow Chard, Pickled Walnut
served with
Harpoon Brewery 100 Barrel Series #57 Sticke Alt
Uinta Brewing Baba

***

Olive Oil Ganache, Salted Caramel, Cherry, Hazelnuts
served with
Port City Brewing COLOSSAL V
Deschutes Brewery The Abyss Rye

UK Train Beers

If you travel by train, it may be useful to know what – arguably – are the best beers in the selections offered by the UK's rail service providers. The following beers are all available as part of their on-board catering service.

Abellio Greater Anglia	Adnams Southwold Bitter
Arriva Trains Wales	Stella Artois
Caledonian Sleeper	Fyne Ales Highlander*
Chiltern Trains	Stella Artois
Cross Country	Black Sheep Ale
East Midlands	Marston's Pedigree
Grand Central	Little Valley Withens Pale Ale
Great Western	St Austell Tribute
Hull Trains	Stella Artois
ScotRail	Belhaven Black
South West Trains	Hall & Woodhouse Tanglefoot
TransPennine Express	Stella Artois
Virgin Trains	RedWillow Tilting Ale

* This fine selection also includes Belhaven Best, Black Isle Goldeneye and Red Kite, Caledonian Deuchars IPA, Fyne Ales Avalanche Ale, Innis & Gunn Original and Lager, and WEST St Mungo Lager.

Note: The following train operators provide no onboard catering: c2c, Gatwick Express, Great Northern, Heathrow Connect/Express, London Midland, Merseyrail, Northern Rail, Southeastern, Southern Trains, Thameslink.

London Hops to It

If you're quick and in London in mid-May, you can sample a rare delicacy when some of the city's most adventurous chefs turn their hands to creating dishes that feature hop shoots. Members of the London Brewers' Alliance make great efforts to gather in the shoots that would otherwise wither on the bine as part of the cultivation process and then deliver them to pubs and restaurants in the capital for use in hop cuisine. Restaurants are also encouraged to find the right beer pairings for the food they prepare. In 2016, more than 40 venues took delivery of the prized shoots, which have been described by some as 'the most expensive vegetable in the world'.

CAMRA's Champion Beers of Scotland and Wales

	Scotland	*Wales*
1996	Caledonian 80/-	Plassey Dragon's Breath
1997	Caledonian 80/-	Plassey Dragon's Breath
1998	Caledonian Deuchars IPA	Flannery's Oatmeal Stout
1999	Harviestoun Bitter & Twisted	Bullmastiff Gold
2000	Orkney Dark Island	Bullmastiff Gold
2001	Inveralmond Ossian's Ale	Tomos Watkin Merlin's Stout
2002	Harviestoun Bitter & Twisted	Bryncelyn Buddy Marvellous
2003	Orkney Dark Island	Bryncelyn Oh Boy
2004	Cairngorm Trade Winds	Breconshire Golden Valley
2005	Cairngorm Black Gold	Bullmastiff Son of a Bitch
2006	Kelburn Cart Blanche	Otley O8
2007	Highland Dark Munro	Rhymney Dark
2008	Highland Scapa Special	Otley O8
2009	Orkney Raven Ale	Purple Moose Snowdonia Ale
2010	Highland Orkney Blast	Otley O-Garden
2011	Isle of Skye Cuillin Beast	Rhymney Dark
2012	Highland Orkney Best	Heart of Wales High as a Kite
2013	Fyne Ales Jarl	Tiny Rebel Dirty Stop Out
2014	Kelburn Dark Moor	Tiny Rebel Fubar
2015	Cairngorm Black Gold	Vale of Glamorgan Dark Matter
2016	Tryst Raj IPA	

Pigs and Hops

The saying 'to buy a pig in a poke', meaning to acquire an item without seeing it first, may actually come from the hop industry, as a 'poke' – probably from the old French 'poche', or pocket – is a type of sack typically used for holding bushels of hops while they await drying. On the other hand, pokes have also had a traditional use in the wool trade, so the phrase may come from that.

Strange Brew

Just when you think brewers can't possibly come up with anything more unusual, they end up surprising you again. The list below highlights some novel creations from particularly adventurous breweries around the world.

Brewery	Beer (ingredients, if not obvious)
3 Sheeps (US)	Nimble Lips Noble Tongue (squid ink)
Angel City (US)	Avocado Ale
Aqula (Japan)	Wild Rice Amber Ale
Belvoir (UK)	Blue Brew (Stilton whey)
Brains (UK)	A-Pork-Alypse (double chocolate bacon porter)
Brussels Beer Project (Belgium)	Baby Lone (waste bread)
	Tante Tatin (apples)
Clown Shoes (US)	Genghis Pecan Pie Porter
Dock Street (US)	Walker (goats' brains)
Four Hearts (Australia)	Wabbit Season (carrots)
Freetail (US)	Spirulina Wit (blue-green algae)
Hawkshead (UK)	Tonka (tonka beans and cacao nibs)
Lost Industry (UK)	Mojito Sour (lactose, lime and mint)
Magic Rock (UK)	Salty Kiss (gooseberries and sea buckthorn)
New Belgium (US)	Coconut Curry Hefeweizen
Rogue (US)	Voodoo (doughnut bacon maple ale)
Short's (US)	Bloody Beer (tomatoes and other bloody Mary ingredients)
Smisje (Belgium)	Big Bayou (Cajun spices)
	Wostyntje (mustard)
TailGate (US)	Peanut Butter Milk Stout
The Lost Abbey (US)	Gift of the Magi (frankincense and myrrh)
Thornbridge (UK)	Rhubarbe de Saison
Wild Beer (UK)	Millionaire (chocolate and salted caramel milk stout)
Wynkoop (US)	Rocky Mountain Oyster Stout (bull testicles)
Yeastie Boys (NZ)	Gunnamatta (Earl Grey tea)

Beer Writers of the Year

The British Guild of Beer Writers was founded in 1988 with the aim of improving the quality and quantity of writing about beer in the media. Its membership is open to book authors, print journalists, online writers, broadcasters, PR professionals, photographers and illustrators. The Guild presents the Beer Writer of the Year awards at a dinner every December.

1988	Allan McLean	2002	Michael Jackson
1989	Michael Jackson	2003	Martyn Cornell
1990	Allan McLean	2004	Ben McFarland
1991	Michael Hardman	2005	Alastair Gilmour
1992	Allan McLean	2006	Ben McFarland
1993	Brian Glover	2007	Alastair Gilmour
1994	Roger Protz	2008	Zak Avery
1995	Andrew Jefford	2009	Pete Brown
1996	Michael Jackson	2010	Simon Jenkins
1997	Roger Protz	2011	Ben McFarland
1998	Alastair Gilmour	2012	Pete Brown
1999	Andrew Jefford	2013	Will Hawkes
2000	Alastair Gilmour	2014	Jessica Boak & Ray Bailey
2001	Jeff Evans	2015	Breandán Kearney

CAMRA's Biggest Beer Festivals

	Festival	Attendance
1	Great British Beer Festival	45,000
2	Cambridge	37,500
3	Peterborough	27,100
4	Nottingham	21,000
5	Chelmsford (summer)	20,900
6	Norwich	18,700
7	National Winter Ales Festival	13,400
8	Reading	13,200
9	Manchester Beer & Cider Festival	12,800
10	Ealing	12,000

Figures shown are for 2015/16, rounded to nearest hundred.

A Concise Guide to International Beer Styles

Helles   4.7–5.3%   Golden
This is what you get if you ask for 'a beer' in Bavaria. This pale lager is noted for its sweet malt flavours and delicate balance of hops that bring herbal notes and sometimes hints of lemon.

Pilsner   4.4–5.8%   Golden
The beer style that has taken over the world but has become somewhat debased along the way. The original pilsner lager came from the town of Pilsen in the Czech Republic. It is typically creamy and full-bodied with a powerful herbal hop character. German pilsner, or pils, is drier and leaner, with a more perfumed hop note, and northern German pilsners are drier again.

Märzen   5.8–6.4%   Amber
Created before pilsner and a stepping stone from the dark lagers that existed before, 'March beer' is a German invention with a fuller body than helles and less crispness than a pilsner. The slightly richer malt character may bring hints of toffee and bread. It is traditionally associated with the Oktoberfest in Munich but modern Oktoberfest beers tend to be paler in colour than true märzen.

Dunkel   4.5–5.5%   Ruby-brown
The Bavarian dark lager. The Munich malt used develops subtle notes of treacle and raisin that are countered by firm but restrained hopping. The long lagering period ensures a lightness of body. Schwarzbier, a speciality of eastern Germany, is a very dark lager with a more bitter roasted grain flavour, perhaps giving smoky notes of dark chocolate and coffee.

Vienna   4.5–5.5%   Amber-red
Like märzen, Vienna predates golden lagers. The Vienna malt on which it is based can bring notes of nut, biscuit and caramel.

Bock   6.5–7%   Golden to dark brown
Bock is a strong, full-bodied lager, with a fairly sweet, full malt profile that just overshadows the herbal, sometimes lemony flavours of the hops. Stronger versions (generally 7% and up) are labelled doppelbock and these may have a fruitier note, particularly raisin in the darker examples.

Weizen or Weissbier 5–5.5%   Cloudy yellow/orange

A Bavarian-origin beer made with a high proportion of wheat alongside barley malt. This gives the beer a bready texture and leaves proteins in suspension, along with some yeast, to give a cloudy appearance (such examples are specifically known as 'hefeweissbier', while filtered versions that pour clear are called 'kristallweissbier'). The beer is only moderately hopped, meaning that the cracker-like wheat notes shine through along with complex fruit and spice notes developed during fermentation by the special yeast. A typical weizen therefore may be bittersweet and filled with flavours such as banana, clove, vanilla and apple. Stronger versions are known as weizenbocks, while darker examples, including some roasted malts that bring notes of caramel and chocolate, are sold as dunkelweizen/dunkelweissbier. All versions are well carbonated.

Berliner Weisse   3%   Pale golden

A deliberately sour wheat beer, thanks to the influence of *Lactobacillus* bacteria, with tart acidic flavours and lemon often to the fore. Germans like it with a dash of fruity or herbal syrup to take away the sharpness.

Gose   4.2–4.8%   Hazy golden

Gose, an eastern German style, has come back from the dead in recent years. Another beer with a high wheat content, it has a sweet-sour flavour underpinned by a delicate sensation of salt, which is added, along with coriander, during the brewing process.

Witbier   4.5–5%   Cloudy yellow

Meaning 'white beer' in Flemish, this Belgian speciality is another beer containing a sizeable quantity of wheat that adds to the turbid appearance. The other distinctive feature is the addition of fruit and spices, most commonly bitter orange peel and coriander, meaning that hops are well underplayed and the beer is bittersweet, peppery and fragrant. Known as bière blanche in French.

Saison   5–8%   Golden to dark amber

Originally a farmhouse ale, saison is more of a tradition than a style, with examples varying widely in interpretation, although it is increasingly common to find saisons that are dry, spicy and ultimately bitter. Some include additional spices to complement the action of the saison yeast. A lively carbonation is typical, too.

Bière de Garde   6–8.5%   Golden to dark brown

The French version of a farmhouse ale, generally well matured at the brewery before going on sale (hence the name 'beer that has been kept'). Some are similar in appearance to traditional British bitters, with their rich amber-brown colour and caramel malt notes, but they are stronger and can have complex herbal notes from the French hops. Golden equivalents are now also common. These tend to be sweeter with perhaps a honey-like character.

Kölsch   4.8–5%   Golden

The beer of Cologne, a delicate pale ale that undergoes a period of lagering for crispness. The result is an easy-drinking, fragrant, bittersweet beer with floral and fruity hop notes.

Altbier   4.5–4.8%   Amber to brown

Düsseldorf is the home of altbier (literally 'old beer'). It is another ale that is lagered after fermentation for a slender body. The darker malts infuse the beer with notes of nut and caramel, with hops, often floral, providing good balancing bitterness.

Lambic   5–6%   Golden

This form of Belgian wheat beer is typified by spontaneous fermentation – the process of allowing wild yeast to attack the sugars in the liquid rather than adding brewers' yeast. Throw in a long fermentation and conditioning period in wooden casks that are rich in friendly bacteria, and some skilful blending of vintages, and the result is a tart, almost cidery and winey drink that is served flat. Some lambics (called gueuze) are combined with fresh, younger examples to ensure more carbonation and are refreshing and spritzy. Others are infused with fruit to create kriek (cherry) or frambozen/framboise (raspberry).

Trappist/Abbey   4.5–12%   Golden to dark brown

These beers have origins in holy places, brewed in monasteries for centuries. The strengths vary, as does the use of dark malts. Beers labelled dubbel and quadrupel tend to be brown, with caramel and dark fruit notes, while tripel is golden/amber and more bitter and hoppy. The yeasts used provide a distinctive spiciness and most beers age well in the bottle. Only beers brewed by Trappist monks can be called Trappist beers; commercial brews in the same vein can only be labelled Abbey beers.

Capital Beer: Rome

Five notable beer bars to help you quench your thirst in the Eternal City.

Bir & Fud, Via Benedetta 23, 00153
Beer and food the name promises and pairings are the name of the game in this Trastevere venue. Alternatively, take a drink in the long, narrow bar.

Birra +, Via del Pigneto 105, 00176
Bar opened in 2009 in Rome's trendy Pigneto area, serving eight draught beers and loads of bottles.

Brasserie 4:20, Via Portuense 20, 00153
Cavern-like bar near Porta Portese with stripped-back, industrial décor and a roof garden. More than 40 beers on tap.

Ma Che Siete Venuti A Fà, Via Benedetta 25, 00153
Also known as the Football Pub, this bar – rubbing shoulders with Bir & Fud – features more draughts than bottles but is another must-visit.

Open Baladin, Via degli Specchi 6, 00186
Shrine to beer in the Campo de' Fiori area, featuring produce from the renowned Baladin brewery near Turin and many others (more than 100 Italian artisan beers).

Clare Balding and the Beer Money

In her autobiography, *My Animals and Other Family*, sports broadcaster Clare Balding reveals how her family became beneficiaries of a brewery fortune. The tale concerns one William Bass, a descendent of the original William Bass who founded the Bass brewery in Burton upon Trent in 1777. With no children of his own, Bass (the younger) feared his family name would die out and so asked a nephew to incorporate it into his own name. Captain Peter Hastings – Clare's grandfather – therefore became Captain Peter Hastings-Bass in return for an inheritance that enabled him to buy racing stables at Kingsclere in Hampshire, where Clare's father and brother, Ian and Andrew Balding, have subsequently trained many fine and successful racehorses, including the 1971 Derby winner, Mill Reef.

Beer Magazines and Newspapers

Magazine	Country	Issues*	Contact
Ale Street News	USA	6	alestreetnews.com
All About Beer	USA	6	allaboutbeer.com
Beer & Brewer Magazine	Australia/ New Zealand	4	beerandbrewer.com
Beer Advocate	USA	12	beeradvocate.com/mag
Beer Connoisseur	USA	4	beerconnoisseur.com
Beer	UK	4	camra.org.uk
Beoir	Ireland	2	beoir.org
Belgian Beer & Food	Belgium	4	belgianbeerandfood.com
Bier!	Netherlands	4	birdypublishing.nl
Bières et Plaisirs	Canada	6	bieresetplaisirs.com
Bierpassie	Belgium	4	beerpassion.com
The Brewers Journal	UK	6	brewersjournal.info
Brew Your Own	US	8	byo.com
Brewery History	UK	4	breweryhistory.com/journal
Celebrator Beer News	USA	4	celebrator.com
Draft Magazine	USA	6	draftmag.com
Fermento Birra	Italy	6	fermentobirramagazine.com
Froth	Australia	12	frothbeer.com
Il Mondo della Birra	Italy	12	ilmondodellabirra.it
The Japan Beer Times	Japan	4	japanbeertimes.com
The New Brewer	USA	6	brewersassociation.org
On Tap	South Africa	4	ontapmag.co.za
Original Gravity	UK	6	originalgravitymag.com
Pivo, Bier & Ale	Czech Republic	6	pivobierale.cz
Taps, The Beer Magazine	Canada	6	tapsmagazine.com
What's Brewing†	UK	12	camra.org.uk
Zymurgy†	USA	6	homebrewersassociation.org
Zytholoog†	Belgium	4	zythos.be

* Number of issues per year. † Membership publications for the relevant organisations.

Worldwide Beer Weeks

Month	Country/City/State
March	Italy
April	Tokyo, Japan
May	Luxembourg
	Melbourne, Australia
	Montreal, Canada
	Paris, France
	Shanghai, China
	Vancouver, Canada
June	Auckland, New Zealand
	Madrid, Spain
	Ontario, Canada
July	Berlin, Germany
August	Singapore
September	Milan, Italy
	Toronto, Canada
October	Sydney, Australia
November	Vienna, Austria
	Western Australia

See also UK and American Beer Weeks (pages 16 and 72).

Fuller's Vintage Ale

In 2016, Fuller's made its stock of Vintage Ales available via its online shop. Some editions, because of their rarity, are now sold at premium prices!

Vintage	Price*	Vintage	Price*	Vintage	Price*
1997	£515	2003	£360	2009	£80
1998	£490	2004	£160	2010	£70
1999	£230	2005	£300	2011	£60
2000	£220	2006	£110	2012	£50
2001	£410	2007	£100	2013	£40
2002	£190	2008	£90	2014	£30

Prices correct in August 2016. * 500 ml bottle

The Trappist Breweries

Only the 11 monastic breweries listed below have official sanction from the Vatican to use the term 'Trappist' on their products. To qualify for Trappist accreditation, the beer must be produced within the confines of the abbey; the monks must at least supervise production; and profits can only be used for the upkeep of the abbey buildings and for good causes. Six of the breweries are in Belgium; two are in the Netherlands, and there is now one each in Austria, Italy and the USA. The Abbaye Sainte Marie du Mont des Cats in northern France also sells a Trappist ale, although this is brewed for it by Chimay. Similar beers produced by commercial breweries for other abbeys under licence, or simply as a religious cash-in, cannot be labelled 'Trappist' and therefore may only be known as 'abbey' beers.

Sint Benedictusabdij de Achelse Kluis, Belgium (Achel)
Abbaye Notre-Dame de Scourmont, Belgium (Chimay)
Stift Engelszell, Austria (Engelszell)
Abdij Onze Lieve Vrouw van Koningshoeven, Netherlands (La Trappe)
Abbaye Notre-Dame d'Orval, Belgium (Orval)
Abbaye Notre-Dame de Saint-Rémy, Belgium (Rochefort)
St Joseph's Abbey, USA (Spencer)
Abbazia delle Tre Fontane, Italy (Tre Fontane)
Abdij der Trappisten van Westmalle, Belgium (Westmalle)
Sint-Sixtusabdij van Westvleteren, Belgium (Westvleteren)
Abdij Maria Toevlucht, Netherlands (Zundert)

Our Other Brewery Is in the South Atlantic

Following the Falklands conflict in 1982, Leicestershire brewery Everards opened its own brewhouse on the South Atlantic islands. The Penguin Brewery, as it was known, was said to be the most southerly real ale brewery in the world at the time and remained in operation for three years. It finally closed in 1986 when its manager opted to move to Britain.

Sewer to Brewer

Scientists at the University of Ghent have developed a way of turning urine into drinking water, using solar power, and they are now planning to use the method to provide liquor for making beer. The solar energy fires up a boiler that heats the urine, which is then separated by a membrane into water and the chemicals potassium, nitrogen and phosphorus that can be used for fertiliser. The scientists hope the system, which was trialled at a music festival, with attendees encouraged to 'pee for science', can be scaled up to provide enough water to produce beer.

Chain Pub Ownership

Chain	Owner
All Bar One	Mitchells & Butlers
Bar & Beyond	Deltic Group
Baroosh	McMullen
Beefeater Grill	Whitbread
Belhaven Pubs	Greene King
Brewers Fayre	Whitbread
Brunning & Price	The Restaurant Group
Castle	Mitchells & Butlers
Chef & Brewer	Greene King
Chicagos	Deltic Group
Classic Inns	Stonegate
Common Room	Stonegate
Crown Carveries	Mitchells & Butlers
Eating Inn	Greene King
Ebb & Flow Café Bar	Marston's
Ember Inns	Mitchells & Butlers
Farmhouse Inns	Greene King
Fayre & Square	Greene King
Flame Grill	Greene King
Generous George	Marston's
Good Night Inns	Greene King
Harvester	Mitchells & Butlers
Head of Steam	Camerons
Hog's Head	Stonegate

Hungry Horse	Greene King
Innkeeper's Lodge	Mitchells & Butlers
Inns of Character	Thwaites
John Barras	Greene King
Lloyds No.1	Wetherspoon
Meet and Eat	Greene King
Metropolitan	Greene King
Nicholson's	Mitchells & Butlers
O'Neill's	Mitchells & Butlers
Oak Tree	Mitchells & Butlers
Old English Inns	Greene King
Orchid Pubs	Mitchells & Butlers
Pitcher & Piano	Marston's
Premier Inn	Whitbread
Premium Country Pubs	Mitchells & Butlers
Project William	Everards
Proper Pubs	Stonegate
Revere	Marston's
Scream	Stonegate
Sizzling Pubs	Mitchells & Butlers
Slug & Lettuce	Stonegate
Table Table	Whitbread
Taylor Walker	Greene King
Toby Pub & Carvery	Mitchells & Butlers
Town Pub & Kitchen	Stonegate
Two For One	Marston's
Varsity	Stonegate
Venues	Stonegate
Village Pub & Kitchen	Mitchells & Butlers
Vintage Inns	Mitchells & Butlers
Wacky Warehouse	Greene King
Walkabout	Intertain
Yates	Stonegate

From Tiny Acorns

It started cautiously in 1971 with just four disillusioned young men but in August 2016 CAMRA's membership stood at a remarkable 181,543.

Further Reading

Below is a selection of detailed, important, useful and entertaining books on beer. Some are still in print, others will require more effort to get hold of (see also Five Highly Influential Beer Books, featured on pages 78–9).

100 Belgian Beers to Try Before You Die!, Tim Webb & Joris Pattyn (CAMRA Books, 2008)

300 Beers to Try Before You Die!/300 More Beers to Try Before You Die!, Roger Protz (CAMRA Books, 2005/2013)

500 Beers, Zak Avery (Apple, 2010)

1001 Beers You Must Try Before You Die, editor Adrian Tierney-Jones (Cassell, 2013)

The Ale Trail, Roger Protz (Dobby, 1995)

Amber Gold & Black, Martyn Cornell (History Press, 2010)

An Appetite for Ale, Fiona Beckett & Will Beckett (CAMRA Books, 2007)

Around Amsterdam/Berlin/Bruges/Brussels/London in 80 Beers, various authors (Cogan & Mater, various years)

The Bedside Book of Beer, Barrie Pepper (Alma Books, 1990)

Beer, Michael Jackson (Dorling Kindersley, 1998)

Beer (Eyewitness Guide), various authors (Dorling Kindersley, 2007)

Beer, The Story of the Pint, Martyn Cornell (Headline, 2003)

A Beer a Day, Jeff Evans (CAMRA Books, 2008)

Beer and Food, Mark Dredge (Dog 'n' Bone, 2014)

The Beer & Food Companion, Stephen Beaumont (Jacqui Small, 2015)

The Beer Bible, Jeff Alworth (Workman, 2015)

The Beer Book, Tim Hampson (Dorling Kindersley, 2008)

Beer Companion, Michael Jackson (Mitchell Beazley, 1993)

The Beer Cookbook, Susan Nowak (Faber & Faber, 1999)

Beer for Pete's Sake, Pete Slosberg (Siris Books, 1998)

Beer Glorious Beer, editors Barrie Pepper and Roger Protz (Quiller, 2000)

Beer in the Netherlands, Tim Skelton (Homewood, 2014)

Beers of North America, Bill Yenne (Longmeadow, 1986)

Brew Britannia, The Strange Rebirth of British Beer, Jessica Boak & Ray Bailey (Aurum, 2014)

The Brewing Industry in England, 1700–1830, Peter Mathias (Gregg Revivals, 1993)

Brewing with Wheat, Stan Hieronymus (Brewers Publications, 2010)

The Brewmaster's Table, Garrett Oliver (HarperCollins, 2003)

Britain's Beer Revolution, Roger Protz & Adrian Tierney-Jones (CAMRA Books, 2014)

The British Brewing Industry 1830–1980, TR Gourvish & RG Wilson (Cambridge, 1994)

The CAMRA Guide to London's Best Beer Pubs & Bars, Des de Moor (CAMRA Books, 2015)

CAMRA's 101 Beer Days Out, Tim Hampson (CAMRA Books, 2015)

The Complete Joy of Homebrewing, Charlie Papazian (Harper, 2003)

Craft Beer World, Mark Dredge (Dog 'n' Bone, 2013)

The English Pub, Peter Haydon (Hale, 1994: republished as *Beer and Britannia*, Sutton, 2001)

For the Love of Hops, Stan Hieronymus (Brewers Publications, 2012)

Good Beer Guide, CAMRA (CAMRA Books, annual)

Good Beer Guide Belgium, Tim Webb & Joe Stange (CAMRA Books, 2014)

Good Bottled Beer Guide, Jeff Evans (CAMRA Books, 2013)

Great Beer Guide, Michael Jackson (Dorling Kindersley, 2005)

Great Beers of Belgium, Michael Jackson (Brewers Publications, 2008)

The Great British Beer Book, Roger Protz (Impact, 1987)

The Guinness Book of Traditional Pub Games, Arthur Taylor (Guinness, 1992)

A History of Brewing, HS Corran (David & Charles, 1975)

Hops and Glory, Pete Brown (Macmillan, 2009)

LambicLand, Tim Webb, Chris Pollard & Siobhan McGinn (Cogan & Mater, 2010)

Let Me Tell You About Beer, Melissa Cole (Pavilion, 2011)

Man Walks into a Pub, Pete Brown (Pan, 2003)

The Oxford Companion to Beer, editor Garrett Oliver (Oxford University Press, 2011)

Played at the Pub, Arthur Taylor (English Heritage, 2009)

Prince of Ales, The History of Brewing in Wales, Brian Glover (Alan Sutton, 1993)

Radical Brewing, Randy Mosher (Brewers Publications, 2004)

So You Want to Be a Beer Expert?, Jeff Evans (CAMRA Books, 2015)

The Taste of Beer, Roger Protz (Weidenfeld & Nicolson, 1998)

Tasting Beer, Randy Mosher (Storey, 2009)

Three Sheets to the Wind, Pete Brown (Pan, 2006)

The World Atlas of Beer, Tim Webb & Stephen Beaumont (Mitchell Beazley, 2016)

World Beer Guide, Roger Protz (Carlton, 2009)

World's Best Beers, Ben McFarland (Jacqui Small, 2009)

Index

Author's Acknowledgements

The author wishes to thank the following people for their input and assistance, and apologises to anyone whose valued contribution may have been inadvertently overlooked: Stephen Beaumont, Katie Button, Cathy Clarke, Martyn Cornell, John Cryne, Peter Darby, Des de Moor, Victoria Dele, Ciro Fakhr, Russell Falconer, Rob Ferguson, Eddie Gershon, Tim Hampson, Gary Holmes, Ellie Hudspith, Paddy Johnson, Alison Lock, Rosie Nicholas, Paul Oakley, Sean Paxton, Lotte Peplow, Hugh Ribbans, David Sheen, Bart Watson, Tim Webb and Vanessa Winstone.

Books for Beer Lovers

CAMRA Books, the publishing arm of the Campaign for Real Ale, is the leading publisher of books on beer and pubs. Key titles include:

Good Beer Guide 2017
Editor: Roger Protz

CAMRA's *Good Beer Guide* is fully revised and updated each year and features pubs across the United Kingdom that serve the best real ale. Now in its 44th edition, this pub guide is completely independent with listings based entirely on nomination and evaluation by CAMRA members. This means you can be sure that every one of the 4,500 pubs deserves their place, plus they all come recommended by people who know a thing or two about good beer.

£15.99   ISBN 978 1 85249 335 6

The Year in Beer: 2017 Diary
Discover a beer for every week of the year with CAMRA's *Year in Beer 2017 Diary*. The best beers from around the world are linked to key events and dates through the year, with comprehensive tasting notes. Major anniversaries, religious feasts and important birthdays are highlighted, along with commemorations, carnivals and some more eccentric events.

£9.99   ISBN 978 1 85249 337 0

CAMRA's Beer Anthology
Editor: Roger Protz

Beer is deeply engrained in the culture and history of the British Isles. From the earliest times, the pleasures of ale and beer have been recorded for posterity. Shakespeare, Dickens and Hardy all wrote on the delights of beer and pubs. They are joined today by a small army of writers with a different aim: they are not commenting on beer in passing, as part of a literary endeavour, but are dedicated full time to researching, promoting and championing beer. From bards to biographers to beer bloggers, explore the world of beer as seen through the eyes of writers as diverse as Bill Bryson, William Blake, Douglas Adams, Melissa Cole, Dylan Thomas, Breandán Kearney, James Joyce, Thomas Hardy, Jeff Evans and George Orwell.

£9.99   ISBN 978 1 85249 333 2

London Pub Walks
Bob Steel

CAMRA's pocket-size walking guide to London is back. This fully-revised second edition is packed with interesting new walks, fully updated classic routes from the first edition, new pubs and a selection of trails that take full advantage of London's public transport network. With 30 walks around more than 200 pubs, CAMRA's London Pub Walks enables you to explore the entire city while never being far from a decent pint.

£11.99   ISBN 978 1 85249 336 3

Yorkshire Pub Walks
Bob Steel

CAMRA's Yorkshire Pub Walks guides you round the best of England's largest county, while never straying too far from a decent pint. A practical, pocket-sized guide to some of the best pubs and best walking in Yorkshire, this fully illustrated book features 25 walks around some of Yorkshire's most awe-inspiring National Parks and landscapes, and its most vibrant towns and cities. Full-colour Ordnance Survey maps and detailed route information, plus pub listings with opening hours and details of draught beers, make it the essential guide for anyone wanting a taste of 'God's Own County'.

£9.99   ISBN 978 1 85249 329 5

London's Best Beer, Pubs & Bars
Des de Moor

The essential guide to London beer, completely revised for 2015. London's Best Beer, Pubs & Bars is packed with detailed maps and easy-to-use listings to help you find the best places to enjoy perfect pints in the capital. Laid out by area, the book will be your companion in exploring the best pubs serving the best British and world beers. Additional features include descriptions of London's rich history of brewing and the city's vibrant modern brewing scene, where brewery numbers have more than doubled in the last three years. The venue listings are fully illustrated with colour photographs and include a variety of real ale pubs, bars and other outlets, with detailed information to make planning any excursion quick and easy.

'...meticulously researched and open-minded'
Will Hawkes, The Independent

£12.99   ISBN 978-1-85249-323-36

So You Want to Be a Beer Expert?
Jeff Evans

More people than ever are searching for an understanding of
what makes a great beer, and this book meets that demand
by presenting a hands-on course in beer appreciation, with
sections on understanding the beer styles of the world, beer
flavours, how beer is made, the ingredients, and more.

Uniquely, *So You Want to Be a Beer Expert?* doesn't just relate
the facts, but helps readers reach conclusions for themselves. Key to this are
the interactive tastings that show readers, through their own taste-buds, what
beer is all about. CAMRA's *So You Want to Be a Beer Expert?* is the ideal
book for anyone who wants to further their knowledge and enjoyment of beer.
£12.99   ISBN 978 1 85249 322 6

101 Beer Days Out
Tim Hampson

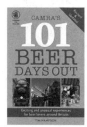

Revised and updated for 2015, *101 Beer Days Out* is the
perfect handbook for the beer tourist wanting to explore
beer, pubs and brewing in the UK. From brewery tours to
rail-ale trails, beer festivals to hop farms, brewing courses
to historic pubs, Britain has a huge variety of beer
experiences to explore and enjoy. *101 Beer Days Out* is
ordered geographically, so you can easily find a beer day
out wherever you are in Britain, and includes full visitor
information, maps and colour photography, with detailed information on
opening hours, local landmarks and public
transport links to make planning any excursion quick and easy.
£12.99   ISBN 978 1 85249 328 8

Britain's Beer Revolution
Roger Protz and Adrian Tierney-Jones

UK brewing has seen unprecedented growth in the last
decade. Breweries of all shapes and sizes are flourishing.
Established brewers applying generations of tradition
in new ways rub shoulders at the bar with new micro-
brewers. Headed by real ale, a 'craft' beer revolution is
sweeping the country. In *Britain's Beer Revolution* Roger
Protz and Adrian Tierney-Jones look behind the beer

labels and shine a spotlight on what makes British beer so good.
£14.99   ISBN 978 1 85249 321 9

Britain's Best Real Heritage Pubs
Geoff Brandwood

This definitive listing is the result of 25 years' research by CAMRA to discover pubs that are either unaltered in 70 years or have features of truly national historic importance. Fully revised, the book boasts updated information and a new set of evocative illustrations. Among the 260 pubs, there are unspoilt country locals, Victorian drinking palaces and mighty roadhouses. The book has features describing how the pub developed, what's distinctive about pubs in different parts of the country, and how people used the pub for take-out sales in the pre-supermarket era. There is a bonus listing of 70 pubs that, while not meeting CAMRA's national criteria for a heritage pub, will still thrill visitors with their historic ambience.
£9.99   ISBN 978 1 85249 334 9

Real Heritage Pubs of the Midlands
Editor: Paul Ainsworth

This guide will lead you to the pubs throughout the East and West Midlands that still have interiors or internal features of real historic significance. They range from rural 'time-warp' pubs, some with no bar counters, to ornate drinking 'palaces' and include some unsung interiors from the inter-war period. The first guide of its kind for the Midlands, it champions the need to celebrate, understand and protect the genuine pub heritage we have left.
£5.99   ISBN 978 1 85249 324 0

Yorkshire's Real Heritage Pubs
Editor: Dave Gamston

This unique guide will lead you to nearly 120 pubs in Yorkshire and Humber which still have interiors or internal features of real historic significance. They range from simple rural 'time-warp' pubs to ornate Victorian drinking 'palaces' and include some of the more unsung pub interiors from the inter-war and later years that we take much for granted.
£4.99   ISBN 978 1 85249 315 8

Order these and other CAMRA books online at **www.camra.org.uk/books**, ask at your local bookstore, or contact:
CAMRA, 230 Hatfield Road, St Albans, AL1 4LW. Telephone 01727 867201

A campaign of two halves

Campaigning for pub goers and beer drinkers

CAMRA, the Campaign for Real Ale, is the not-for-profit independent voice of real ale drinkers and pub goers. CAMRA's vision is to have quality real ale and thriving pubs in every community. We campaign tirelessly to achieve this goal, as well as lobbying government to champion drinkers' rights. As a CAMRA member you will have the opportunity to campaign to save pubs under threat of closure, for pubs to be free to serve a range of real ales at fair prices and for a long-term freeze in beer duty that will help Britain's brewing industry survive.

Enjoying real ale and pubs

CAMRA has over 175,000 members from all ages and backgrounds, brought together by a common belief in the issues that CAMRA deals with and their love of good quality British beer. From just **£24** a year* – that's less than a pint a month – you can join CAMRA and enjoy the following benefits:

- Subscription to *What's Brewing*, our monthly colour newspaper, and *Beer*, our quarterly magazine, informing you about beer and pub news and detailing events and beer festivals around the country.

- Free or reduced entry to over 160 national, regional and local beer festivals.

- Money off many of our publications including the *Good Beer Guide*, the *Good Bottled Beer Guide* and *So You Want to Be a Beer Expert*?

- Access to a members-only section of our website, **www.camra.org.uk**, which gives up-to-the-minute news stories and includes a special offer section with regular features.

- Special discounts with numerous partner organisations and money off real ale in your participating local pubs as part of our Pubs Discount Scheme.

Log onto **www.camra.org.uk/join** for CAMRA membership information.

---

*£24 membership cost stated is only available via Direct Debit, other concessionary rates available.

Please note membership rates stated are correct at the time of printing but are subject to change.

Full details of all membership rates can be found here:
www.camra.org.uk/membershiprates